ABOUT THE AUTHOR

Graduating from the Culinary Institute of America in Hyde Park, NY, Ari Sexner has trained under Michelin star chefs and has worked at numerous 5-star 5-diamond rated resorts and eventually made his way into cold-pressed juice, developing the first unpasteurized USDA Certified Organic juice program in Las Vegas for the Bellagio Hotel.

Taking what he's learned as a chef, Ari has gone on to consult for hundreds of juice and health food companies. He has a passion for guiding founders and managers through kitchen planning, operations, recipe creation, food costing, sourcing ingredients, NSF and HACCP training, SSOP programs, USDA Organic Certification, and more.

THE JUICING COMPANION

By Ari Sexner

Published by Goodnature Products, Inc.

Buffalo, New York, USA

Artwork and design by Chris Vogel

Edited by Robin A. Frey

ISBN: 978-1-7326895-0-3

The material in this publication is of the nature of general comment only, and does not represent professional advice. It is not intended to provide specific guidance for particular circumstances and it should not be relied on as the basis for any decision to take action or not take action on any matter which it covers. Readers should obtain professional advice where appropriate, before making any such decision. To the maximum extent permitted by law, the author and publisher disclaim all responsibility and liability to any person, arising directly or indirectly from any person taking or not taking action based on the information in this publication.

Some of these products or claims have not been scientifically proven to treat, cure, or prevent any disease.

Always make sure when selecting supplements that they are approved for food use by the FDA and/or local health department.

Contents

ACKNOWLEDGMENTS:

I would like to thank my family and friends for putting up with me as well as for all of the support and guidance. My mom, Lori, and brother, Justin, for always pushing me and helping me with the big tough decisions in life. Nina, my fiancé, no matter how bad a day, I always cherish our time together — past, present and future. Chef Brad Skougard, you know you are family to me; you taught me a lot, the best qualities I try to emulate from you are your ability to always stay positive under pressure no matter the circumstance and knowing the true meaning of working in the hospitality industry. Chef Adam Cioffi, my Italian brother, who has taught me many things, but most importantly his family's Sunday gravy recipe. My good friends and co-workers in the kitchen, Chef Robert Moreto and Chef Eric Mistry, I had great times and memories I will never forget working with you both, and I look forward to the day when we can all get together and cook again.

Thanks to the Wettlaufers for having a vision and idea and never giving up on it, as well as giving me the opportunity to do what I love and help others. Charlie Wettlaufer, this never would have happened if you hadn't given me a chance, this chance you gave me has changed my life for the best. Robin Frey, for all the hard work, ideas and long hours put into this book—we couldn't have done this without you. You are always so hard working, organized and thorough with such a positive attitude. Chris Vogel for sorting through the random thoughts and ideas, seeing our vision, and designing something beautiful and refined. Annie Parks from the Balanced Bee Juicery, for always being there to assist with any nutritional / additive questions and educating me on their importance along the way. Last, but definitely not least, the entire Goodnature family, fellow juice bar operators, owners, distributors, team, and supporters: Being able to make a living by providing your community health and wellness is no easy task; your hard work truly changes lives and does not go unnoticed.

– Ari Sexner

FOREWORD

I first met Ari during the time he was the garde manger executive chef at Bellagio Resort in Las Vegas. That means he was in charge of all the cold food for the property, which includes 15 restaurants, banquet halls, villas, an expansive outdoor pool area, and the beautiful 3,000 plus room hotel. He had 40 cooks and 3 chefs working under him, and they prepared food for up to 10,000 meals per day. Ari came to me because the Bellagio decided to add organic certified cold-pressed juice to their offerings, made in-house, and Ari had some questions about Goodnature juice equipment.

At the time, there wasn't a lot of information available about producing juice on a commercial level, so it took Ari nearly two years of research before he was able to finally launch the program. When I took a tour of his setup, it was the most beautiful juicing operation I've seen. All juice was made in a refrigerated room, there were meticulous log books kept for sanitation and organic certification, and everything was clean and spotless. More impressive than that, though, were the amazing juice recipes. A simple yet captivating juice menu, and everything was just right.

I asked Ari if he would consider helping other entrepreneurs that came to Goodnature for help, and he said he would be happy to. When our customers needed help with everything from dealing with the health department to creating recipes, Ari would work with them hand-in-hand to ensure their success in their new venture. The feedback we received from our clients was outstanding, and eventually we recruited him full time to work as Goodnature's official juice consultant. Since then he has worked with hundreds of juice entrepreneurs all over the world.

One of Ari's strengths is the ability to not only help his clients, but to give them the tools they need to help themselves. Without having the background of a culinary education and years of experience dealing with sweetness, acidity, and the taste palate, it can be overwhelming to try to create recipes from scratch. Ari was determined to make it easier for everyone. He came to me with the idea for this book in 2015, and has put hundreds of hours of work into it.

There are plenty of juice recipe books available with thousands of great recipes, but if your desire is to learn how to create your own amazing recipes, this is the only tool you need.

– Charlie Wettlaufer, President of Goodnature Products, Inc.

HOW TO USE THIS BOOK

The purpose of this book is not just to provide recipes, but to enable chefs, juice entrepreneurs, and general juice enthusiasts to develop amazing recipes from scratch.

The concept is simple: Choose a specific ingredient you wish to use in your juice—whether it be based on product availability, planning for the upcoming season's harvest, or you want to consume some extra produce you have laying around—and open to that page in the book (ingredients are in alphabetical order). There, you will find flavor pairings, nutritional information, and recipe ideas to get you started.

This book gives you the following tools to help you be creative:

SEASONALITY LIST

If you're drawing a blank on what to start with, why not try something that's in season and fresh? On the seasonality list, you can determine what's in season right now and use that as your starting ingredient.

FLAVOR PAIRINGS

Flavor pairings are recommended ingredients to combine with your selected starting ingredient to form a base for a recipe. Each flavor pairing ingredient may act as a starting point for additional flavor pairings by finding the corresponding ingredient page in the book.

IDEAS

On each ingredient page you will find some ideas to help you get started. Each idea is made up of a combination of flavor pairings and other ingredients which can be expanded upon to create your own masterpiece.

RECIPES

Although it's fun to create recipes from scratch, sometimes you just need something tried and true. Every eleven pages you will find a recipe that has been taste tested and proven to be delicious. Recipes always build a great foundation, and once you get comfortable with some of these classics, try substituting some of your favorite produce varieties to give it your own twist.

BOOSTERS + ADDITIVES

There are hundreds of ingredients you can add to juice that aren't actually juice. Here we have included the most beneficial items like honey, hemp seeds, and more.

Most importantly, have fun and don't be afraid to try something new. You should always be adventurous when making new recipes, and never stop experimenting. The juicing industry in an exciting place to be, and the best recipes are made with love.

Always wash produce thoroughly and use a produce or antimicrobial wash. When serving a raw, unpasteurized juice, you want to make sure the product is as clean as possible.

If the peel doesn't affect the flavor or color of the juice, don't peel it! There is a large concentration of beneficial nutrients in the outer layer of many fruits and vegetables.

PINEAPPLES

Remove the green crown and cut into quarters, but leave the skin on.

APPLES

You can keep whole and unpeeled.

CUCUMBERS

Clean with antimicrobial wash to remove any wax. For light colored, non-green juices, I peel the cucumbers — otherwise I leave the skin on.

LEMONS & LIMES

For stronger flavored or full bodied juices, grind these with the peel on — this is a preference where some might disagree, but when juiced whole, the peel is not as bitter than it is with oranges and grapefruits.

MELONS

You can either peel or keep the rind on watermelon. If it is not that sweet, we recommend peeling it. De-seed honeydew and cantaloupe, as you get a slightly bitter flavor when you grind or process the seeds.

NUTS

In general, remove shells — however, keep or order with the skins on if possible, nuts such as almonds contain a lot of flavor in the brown skin.

PASSION FRUIT

In most areas these are a bit pricey, I like to add this to finished juice by scooping out the seeds and mixing them into the juice.

PREP

PRO

FOR

RING

UCE

UICE

BEETS

Remove the top ends and clean the bottoms thoroughly. If they are small in size, remove the bottom root as well.

BERRIES

These small, fleshy fruits have a soft texture and do not contain a lot of liquid. Blend into a puree or juice using an auger style juicer, and then add it to the juice.

LEAFY VEGETABLES

In general, do not remove the stems, as they typically contain a lot of flavor and juice. Coming from the farm, leafy greens usually have the most dirt on the leaves and need to be thoroughly washed.

ORANGES & GRAPEFRUITS

Peel these citrus fruits due to the bitter flavor of the pith.

CARROTS

Remove the top ends of the carrots due to the fact that it's tough to remove all the dirt.

MANGOES & PAPAYAS

These are a little pricey in most locations and do not contain a lot of juice – I recommend to blend in a blender or juice using an auger style juicer, and then add to the juice.

If the seeds are the size of a cherry pit or larger, remove them. Pits and large seeds can lend a slightly bitter flavor to juice, as well as wear down or even damage blades.

For large items (pineapples and larger), we prefer to cut into quarters. This will make it easier to process the produce at a more consistent rate.

SEASONAL AV

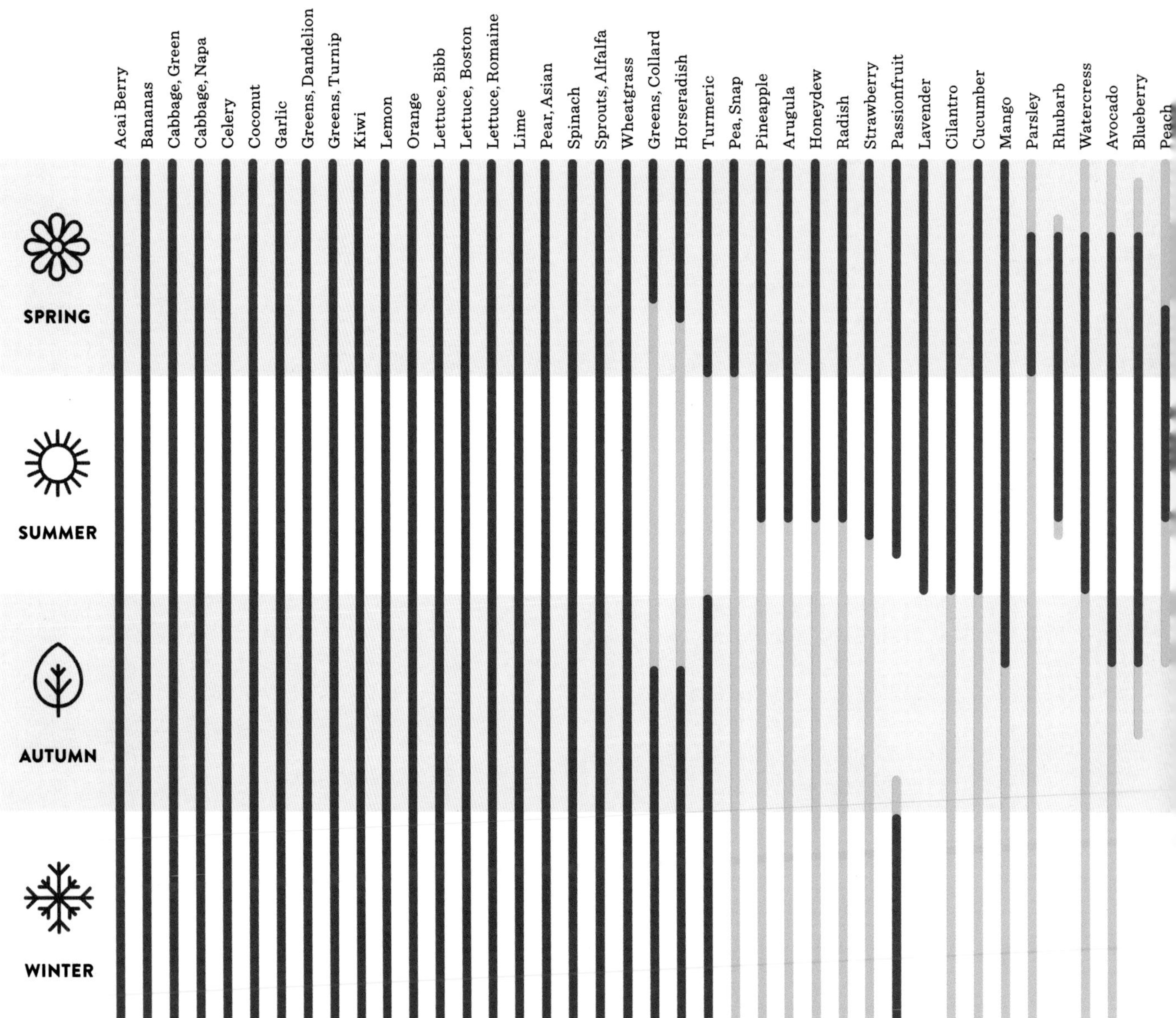
Acai Berry
Bananas
Cabbage, Green
Cabbage, Napa
Celery
Coconut
Garlic
Greens, Dandelion
Greens, Turnip
Kiwi
Lemon
Orange
Lettuce, Bibb
Lettuce, Boston
Lettuce, Romaine
Lime
Pear, Asian
Spinach
Sprouts, Alfalfa
Wheatgrass
Greens, Collard
Horseradish
Turmeric
Pea, Snap
Pineapple
Arugula
Honeydew
Radish
Strawberry
Passionfruit
Lavender
Cilantro
Cucumber
Mango
Parsley
Rhubarb
Watercress
Avocado
Blueberry
Peach
SPRING
SUMMER
AUTUMN
WINTER

ILABILITY

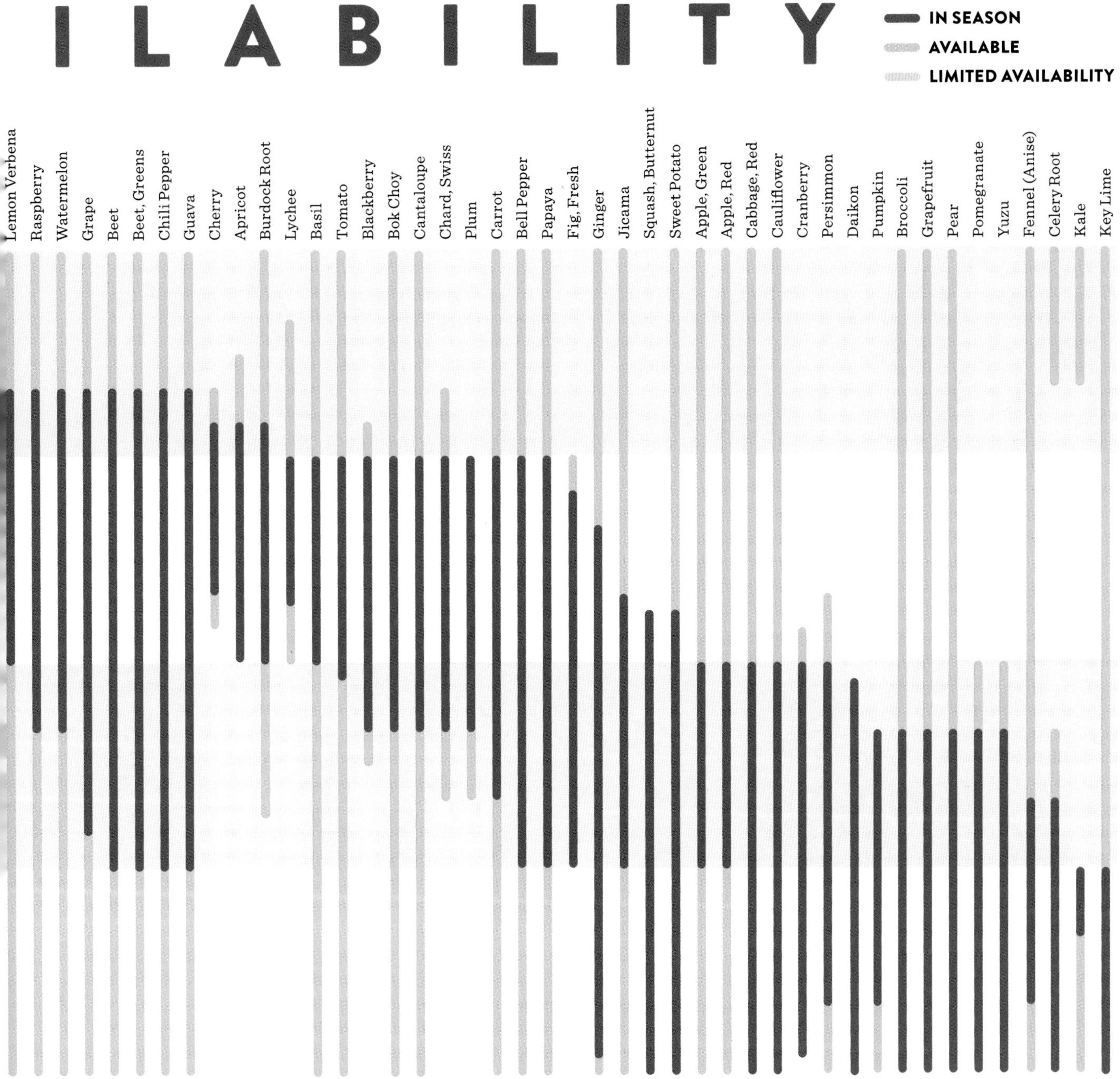

IN SEASON
AVAILABLE
LIMITED AVAILABILITY

Lemon Verbena
Raspberry
Watermelon
Grape
Beet
Beet, Greens
Chili Pepper
Guava
Cherry
Apricot
Burdock Root
Lychee
Basil
Tomato
Blackberry
Bok Choy
Cantaloupe
Chard, Swiss
Plum
Carrot
Bell Pepper
Papaya
Fig, Fresh
Ginger
Jicama
Squash, Butternut
Sweet Potato
Apple, Green
Apple, Red
Cabbage, Red
Cauliflower
Cranberry
Persimmon
Daikon
Pumpkin
Broccoli
Grapefruit
Pear
Pomegranate
Yuzu
Fennel (Anise)
Celery Root
Kale
Key Lime

A
B
C
D
E
F
G
H
I
J
K
L
M
N
O
P
Q
R
S
T
U
V
W
X
Y
Z

Acai Berry *(frozen puree)*

IN SEASON
AVAILABLE
LIMITED AVAILABILITY

SUB CATEGORY: FRUIT, BERRY

HEALTH BENEFITS

Promotes cardiovascular health, digestive health, antioxidant, helps immune system, promotes weight loss

FLAVOR PAIRING

Agave Nectar
Almond
Banana
Blueberry
Chocolate
Coconut
Goji Berry
Honey
Maple Syrup
Mint
Nuts
Pomegranate
Raspberry
Strawberry
Yogurt
Vanilla

IDEAS

1. **ACAI BERRY + VANILLA + YOGURT + HONEY**
2. **ACAI BERRY + BANANA + BERRIES**
3. **ACAI BERRY + POMEGRANATE + MAPLE SYRUP + AGAVE NECTAR**

SEASON

Year-round

FLAVOR

Deep berry flavor with slight hints of earthiness with semi sweet notes

PROCESSING

Best for juices when thawed and whisked in or blended for either smoothies or acai bowls

CONTAINS

Vitamin A

Almond

SUB CATEGORY: NUT

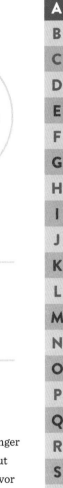

IN SEASON
AVAILABLE
LIMITED AVAILABILITY

HEALTH BENEFITS

Promotes weight loss, lowers blood pressure, lowers cholesterol, antioxidant, lowers blood sugar, improves cardiovascular health, helps with type 2 diabetes

SEASON

Year-round

FLAVOR

Nutty, slightly sweet

FLAVOR PAIRING

Agave Nectar
Apple
Apricot
Banana
Berries
Carrot
Cherry
Chocolate
Cacao Nib
Cinnamon
Coconut
Coffee
Date
Fig
Ginger
Grape
Hazelnut
Honey
Lavender
Maple Syrup
Molasses
Peach
Pear
Pecan
Pistachio
Raisin
Rose Water
Vanilla
Yogurt

PROCESSING

Toasting almonds will bring out different stronger flavor, perfect nut for nut mylks, due to strong flavor

CONTAINS

Calcium, Iron, Vitamin E

IDEAS

1. ALMOND + DATE + VANILLA
2. ALMOND + DRIED FIG + LAVENDER
3. ALMOND + MAPLE SYRUP + CINNAMON
4. ALMOND + PISTACHIO + HONEY + ROSE WATER

A B C D E F G H I J K L M N O P Q R S T U V W X Y Z

Aloe Vera

IN SEASON
AVAILABLE
LIMITED AVAILABILITY

SUB CATEGORY: VEGETABLE

HEALTH BENEFITS

Aids digestion, detoxification, improves cardiovascular health, reduces inflammation, hydrates

FLAVOR PAIRING

Due to its neutral flavor, can be incorporated or blended in almost all juices

IDEAS

1. ALOE VERA + COCONUT WATER + MINT
2. ALOE VERA + PINEAPPLE + CUCUMBER
3. ALOE VERA + MAPLE SYRUP + CINNAMON

SEASON

Year-round

FLAVOR

Neutral flavor

PROCESSING

Remove the gel from the aloe vera plant by first trimming the sides, then cut lengthwise to split leaf, scrape using a spoon, be sure not to scrape too deep, if the gel is slightly yellow you have scraped too close to the outside layer.

CONTAINS

Minerals, Amino acids, Alkalinity

Apple, Green

SUB CATEGORY: FRUIT

— IN SEASON
— AVAILABLE
— LIMITED AVAILABILITY

HEALTH BENEFITS

Helps prevent Alzheimer's disease, anti-inflammatory, antioxidant, helps with asthma, lowers blood fat levels, lowers blood sugar levels, strengthens bones, prevents some forms of cancers, improves cardiovascular health, lowers cholesterol, helps with constipation, improves digestive tract, increases energy, helps with heart disease, improves immune system, reduces inflammation, increases metabolism, aids weight loss

FLAVOR PAIRING

Agave Nectar	Cayenne	Date	Lavender	Raisin
Allspice	Celery	Fennel	Maple Syrup	Rhubarb
Almond	Celery Root	Fig	Mint	Rosemary
Apricot	Cherry	Ginger	Molasses	Sweet Potato
Banana	Chili Pepper	Grape	Nutmeg	Vanilla
Beet	Cilantro	Greens	Parsnip	Watermelon
Berries	Cinnamon	Honey	Pear	Yogurt
Cardamom	Citrus	Honeydew	Pineapple	
Carrot	Clove	Jicama	Pumpkin	
Cashew	Coconut	Kale	Quince	

IDEAS

1. GREEN APPLE + KALE + CELERY + CUCUMBER + LEMON + GINGER
2. GREEN APPLE + HONEYDEW + LIME + MINT
3. GREEN APPLE + PINEAPPLE + MINT

SEASON

Year-round especially in autumn

FLAVOR

Tart and sweet with a crisp acidity

PROCESSING

The skin is high in antioxidants, flavor pairing green juices where the sweet, crisp, tartness will balance the flavor.

CONTAINS

Vitamin C, Potassium

Apple, Red Variety

IN SEASON
AVAILABLE
LIMITED AVAILABILITY

SUB CATEGORY: **FRUIT**

HEALTH BENEFITS

Helps prevent Alzheimer's disease, anti-inflammatory, antioxidant, helps with asthma, lowers blood fat levels, lowers blood sugar levels, strengthens bones, prevents some forms of cancers, improves cardiovascular health, lowers cholesterol, helps with constipation, improves digestive tract, increases energy, helps with heart disease, improves immune system, reduces inflammation, increases metabolism, aids weight loss

FLAVOR PAIRING

Agave Nectar	Cayenne	Date	Molasses	Vanilla
Allspice	Celery	Fennel	Nutmeg	Yogurt
Almond	Celery Root	Fig	Parsnip	
Apricot	Cherry	Ginger	Pear	
Banana	Chili Pepper	Grape	Pumpkin	
Beet	Cilantro	Honey	Quince	
Berries	Cinnamon	Jicama	Raisin	
Cardamom	Citrus	Lavender	Rhubarb	
Carrot	Clove	Maple Syrup	Rosemary	
Cashew	Coconut	Mint	Sweet Potato	

IDEAS

1. RED APPLE + CARROT + LEMON + GINGER
2. RED APPLE + RED BEET + GINGER + LEMON + PEAR
3. RED APPLE + CINNAMON + ORANGE + CLOVE + NUTMEG
4. RED APPLE + SWEET POTATO + LEMON + MOLASSES + PUMPKIN SPICE BLEND

SEASON

Year-round especially in autumn

FLAVOR

Semi sweet flavor with a floral aroma

PROCESSING

The skin is high in antioxidants, mix different varieties of red apples to get the perfect level of sweetness in your juice

CONTAINS

Vitamin C, Potassium

Apricot

SUB CATEGORY: FRUIT

IN SEASON
AVAILABLE
LIMITED AVAILABILITY

HEALTH BENEFITS

Prevents anemia, antioxidant, helps with cataracts, lowers cholesterol, aids digestion, prevents diverticulosis, improves eyesight, prevents heart disease, increases hemoglobin, prevents macular degeneration, promotes healthy skin

FLAVOR PAIRING

Agave Nectar
Almond
Apple
Arugula
Basil
Beet
Berries
Cardamom
Carrot
Cherry
Cilantro
Cinnamon
Clove
Coconut
Fennel
Fig
Ginger
Grapefruit
Honey
Lemon
Lemongrass
Lime
Mango
Maple Syrup
Mint
Nutmeg
Orange
Peach
Pecan
Pineapple
Pistachio
Raisin
Tarragon
Thyme
Vanilla
Yogurt

IDEAS

1. APRICOT + ORANGE + PINEAPPLE
2. APRICOT + MINT + MANGO + YOGURT
3. APRICOT + STRAWBERRY + HONEY + VANILLA + YOGURT

SEASON

Summer

FLAVOR

Sour and sweet with hints of honey and peaches

PROCESSING

De-seed and can be juiced but works best blended into juice or a smoothie

CONTAINS

Vitamin A, Vitamin C

Aronia Berry *(frozen puree)*

IN SEASON
AVAILABLE
LIMITED AVAILABILITY

SUB CATEGORY: **FRUIT**

HEALTH BENEFITS

Antioxidant packed, improves blood circulation, anti-inflammatory

FLAVOR PAIRING

Acai
Agave Nectar
Almond
Banana
Blueberry
Chocolate
Coconut
Goji Berry
Honey
Maple Syrup
Mint
Nuts
Pomegranate
Raspberry
Strawberry
Yogurt
Vanilla

IDEAS

1. ARONIA BERRY + CRANBERRY + RED APPLE
2. ARONIA BERRY + VANILLA + YOGURT + HONEY
3. ARONIA BERRY + STRAWBERRY + RASPBERRY + AGAVE NECTAR + MINT + YOGURT

SEASON

Year-round

FLAVOR

Deep berry astringent flavor with sweet and sour notes

PROCESSING

Also known as a chokeberry, typically found either in flash frozen form or powder, works well as both being juiced or added to smoothies

CONTAINS

Iron, Vitamin C, Vitamin E

Arugula

SUB CATEGORY: **VEGETABLE, LETTUCE**

— IN SEASON
— AVAILABLE
— LIMITED AVAILABILITY

A B C D E F G H I J K L M N O P Q R S T U V W X Y Z

HEALTH BENEFITS

Promotes eye health, strengthens heart, improves immune system, prevents some forms of cancer, prevents osteoporosis, helps with type 2 diabetes, aids weight loss

FLAVOR PAIRING

Apple	Fennel	Lime	Tomato
Apricot	Fig	Maple Syrup	
Avocado	Garlic	Melon	
Basil	Ginger	Mint	
Beet	Grapefruit	Peach	
Bell Pepper	Greens	Pear	
Carrot	Honey	Pea	
Cilantro	Horseradish	Pomegranate	
Cucumber	Jicama	Spinach	
Daikon	Lettuce	Squash	

IDEAS

1. ARUGULA + PEAR + BEET + HONEY + ORANGE
2. ARUGULA + PINEAPPLE + GREEN APPLE + MINT
3. ARUGULA + TOMATO + CELERY + GARLIC + CUCUMBER + HORSERADISH

SEASON

Year-round especially spring through summer

FLAVOR

Hot and peppery with notes of pepper and horseradish

PROCESSING

Works well in juices as spicy component similar to black pepper

CONTAINS

Vitamin A, Vitamin C, Vitamin K, Manganese, Magnesium

Avocado

IN SEASON
AVAILABLE
LIMITED AVAILABILITY

SUB CATEGORY: **VEGETABLE**

HEALTH BENEFITS

Anti-inflammatory, antioxidant, helps prevent arthritis, lowers blood sugar, lowers blood pressure, strengthens cardiovascular system, promotes eye health, improves immune system, prevents kidney stones, helps with morning sickness, increases muscle strength, improves nervous system, prevents osteoarthritis, prevents psoriasis, helps with rheumatoid arthritis, prevents ulcers

FLAVOR PAIRING

Arugula
Basil
Beet
Bell pepper
Carrot
Cashew
Celery
Chili Pepper
Cilantro
Cucumber
Fennel
Garlic
Ginger
Grapefruit
Greens
Lemon
Lettuce
Lime
Mango
Melon
Orange
Parsley
Pear
Persimmon
Pomegranate
Spinach
Tomato
Yogurt

IDEAS

1. AVOCADO + BANANA + ALMOND MYLK + HONEY
2. AVOCADO + CARROT + SPINACH + TOMATO + CUCUMBER
3. AVOCADO + MANGO + YOGURT + CINNAMON + CAYENNE + AGAVE NECTAR

SEASON

Year-round especially spring through summer

FLAVOR

Creamy buttery taste with light hints of nuts and fruit

PROCESSING

Works great as an emulsifier for savory or slightly sweet smoothies, great substitute for dairy in smoothies

CONTAINS

Vitamin K, Vitamin C, Potassium, Vitamin B9-Folate, Vitamin C

Banana

— IN SEASON
— AVAILABLE
— LIMITED AVAILABILITY

SUB CATEGORY: FRUIT

HEALTH BENEFITS

Prevents anemia, anti-inflammatory, antioxidant, prevents atherosclerosis, lowers blood pressure, strengthens bones, brain food, prevents some forms of cancers, improves cardiovascular health, prevents diabetes, improves digestive system, increases energy, promotes fat burning, strengthens intestines, improves kidney function, helps with morning sickness, prevents muscle cramps, improves muscular function, relieves stress, prevents strokes, prevents ulcers

FLAVOR PAIRING

Agave Nectar
Apple
Berries
Cardamom
Cherry
Chilies
Chocolate
Cinnamon
Citrus
Coconut
Date
Fig
Flaxseed
Ginger
Honey
Lemon
Lime
Mango
Maple Syrup
Orange
Papaya
Peach
Pear
Pineapple
Raisin
Sunflower Seed
Sweet Potato
Tamarind
Tropical Fruit
Vanilla
Yogurt
Yuzu

IDEAS

1. BANANA + STRAWBERRY + YOGURT + HONEY
2. BANANA + PEANUT BUTTER + CHOCOLATE + HONEY
3. BANANA + MANGO + CINNAMON + CAYENNE + LIME + YOGURT

SEASON

Year-round

FLAVOR

Sweet and firm with a creamy texture with floral notes

PROCESSING

Great universal emulsifier for smoothies

CONTAINS

Potassium, Vitamin B6, Vitamin C, Manganese

Recipe

GREEN HERB BLEND

INGREDIENTS

CUCUMBER 28.6%
7.2oz / 205g

GREEN APPLE 22.4%
5.7oz / 160g

WATERCRESS 14.4%
3.6oz / 103g

KALE 14.3%
3.6oz / 103g

ROMAINE 9.6%
2.4oz/ 69g

LEMON 4.9%
3.6oz / 103g

CILANTRO 1.9%
0.48oz/ 14g

PARSLEY 1.9%
0.48oz/ 14g

MINT 1.9%
0.48oz/ 14g

BENEFITS

1. *Antioxidant rich*
2. *Skin purifying*
3. *Reduces cholesterol*

RECIPE YIELD

16 oz / 473 ml

FLAVOR PROFILE

SWEET — SAVORY

LIGHT — BOLD

FRUIT — VEGGIE

Basil

SUB CATEGORY: HERB

— IN SEASON
— AVAILABLE
— LIMITED AVAILABILITY

HEALTH BENEFITS

Anti-inflammatory, improves cardiovascular health, increases bone strength

FLAVOR PAIRING

Almond
Avocado
Bell Pepper
Cauliflower
Cilantro
Cucumber
Garlic
Ginger
Hazelnut
Jicama
Kale
Lemon
Marjoram
Mint
Nuts
Parsley
Peach
Pea
Pine nut
Pistachio
Rosemary
Snap Pea
Spinach
Squash
Sweet Potato
Tomato
Watermelon

IDEAS

1. **BASIL + WATERMELON + CUCUMBER**
2. **BASIL + LEMON + AGAVE NECTAR + WATER**
3. **BASIL + LEMON + TOMATO + GARLIC + CELERY + CUCUMBER + SALT**

SEASON

Year -round especially during summer

FLAVOR

Fragrant with pungent herbal floral notes

PROCESSING

When juicing use stems and leaves together, can be used to add herbal notes to both sweet and savory combinations

CONTAINS

Vitamin K, Manganese

A B C D E F G H I J K L M N O P Q R S T U V W X Y Z

Beet

SUB CATEGORY: **VEGETABLE, ROOT**

HEALTH BENEFITS

Aids in digestion, increases energy, lowers blood pressure, increases mental strength, prevents some forms of cancer, anti-inflammatory

FLAVOR PAIRING

Agave Nectar
Allspice
Apple
Arugula
Avocado
Basil
Bell Pepper
Berries
Cabbage
Cardamom
Carrot
Celery
Celery Root
Chard
Chili Pepper
Chocolate
Cilantro
Cinnamon
Citrus
Clove
Cucumber
Fennel
Ginger
Greens
Honey
Kale
Lavender
Lemon
Lettuce
Lime
Mango
Maple Syrup
Mint
Nutmeg
Orange
Parsley
Pears
Pomegranate
Spinach
Star Anise
Tarragon
Tomato
Wasabi
Watercress
Watermelon
Yogurt

IDEAS

1. **BEET + PEAR + LEMON + GINGER**
2. **BEET + ORANGE + CUCUMBER + KALE**
3. **BEET + TOMATO + CILANTRO + GARLIC + TURMERIC + CELERY + CUCUMBER + JALAPEÑO**

SEASON

Year-round especially summer through autumn

FLAVOR

Sweet flavor with pungent earthy notes

PROCESSING

Pick your variety of beet based on matching the color to your juice, remove very top and bottom prior to juicing as they are extremely difficult to clean completely, you can also add a small amount of beet to enhance the color of a juice

CONTAINS

Vitamin B9-Folate, Manganese, Potassium, Vitamin C, Iron, Copper

Beet, Greens *(tops)*

SUB CATEGORY: **VEGETABLE, LETTUCE**

HEALTH BENEFITS

Aids in digestion, increases energy, lowers blood pressure, increases mental strength, prevents some forms of cancer, anti-inflammatory

FLAVOR PAIRING

Apple	Greens
Banana	Hazelnut
Beet	Horseradish
Cabbage	Kale
Celery	Lemon
Chard	Orange
Cucumber	Yogurt
Fig	
Garlic	
Ginger	

IDEAS

1. BEET GREENS + CUCUMBER + ORANGE
2. BEET GREENS + APPLES + YOGURT + HONEY + BANANA
3. BEET GREENS + KALE + CELERY + CUCUMBER + GREEN APPLE + LEMON + GINGER

IN SEASON
AVAILABLE
LIMITED AVAILABILITY

SEASON

Year-round especially summer through autumn

FLAVOR

Bitter and slightly sweet with earthy notes of cabbage

PROCESSING

Packed with nutrients, can give unique beet type flavor to green juices

CONTAINS

Vitamin A, Vitamin C, Vitamin K, Vitamin B2, Vitamin B6, Vitamin B1, Calcium, Potassium, Vitamin E, Iron, Magnesium, Copper, Manganese

Bell Pepper

IN SEASON
AVAILABLE
LIMITED AVAILABILITY

SUB CATEGORY: VEGETABLE, LETTUCE

HEALTH BENEFITS

Aids in digestion, increases energy, lowers blood pressure, increases mental strength, prevents some forms of cancer, anti-inflammatory

FLAVOR PAIRING

Anise	Chili Pepper	Lemon
Arugula	Cilantro	Lime
Basil	Cucumber	Mango
Bok Choy	Fennel	Mint
Broccoli	Garlic	Parsley
Cabbage	Ginger	Pear
Carrots	Greens	Pineapple
Cayenne	Honey	Snap Pea
Celery	Jicama	Squash
Chard	Kale	Sweet Potato

IDEAS

1. **BELL PEPPER + CELERY + TOMATO + LEMON + CUCUMBER**
2. **BELL PEPPER, GREEN + CUCUMBER + KALE + BASIL + LIME + GINGER**
3. **BELL PEPPER, RED + SWEET POTATO + CARROT + ORANGE + GINGER**

SEASON

Peak summer through autumn

FLAVOR

Sweet, fresh, crisp flavor with slight peppery notes

PROCESSING

Removing seeds is optional when juicing, can tend to get slightly bitter occasionally, select different varieties to alter the color of the juice

CONTAINS

Vitamin C, Vitamin B6, Vitamin A, Vitamin B9-Folate

Blackberry

SUB CATEGORY: **FRUIT, BERRY**

— IN SEASON
— AVAILABLE
— LIMITED AVAILABILITY

HEALTH BENEFITS

Antioxidant, prevents some forms of cancer, promotes healthy skin, anti-inflammatory, increases brain health, increases oral health

FLAVOR PAIRING

Almond
Apple
Banana
Blueberry
Cinnamon
Fig
Ginger
Honey
Lemon
Lime
Mango
Maple Syrup
Melon
Mint
Nutmeg
Orange
Papaya
Pecan
Peach
Raspberry
Strawberry
Vanilla
Watermelon
Yogurt

IDEAS

1. BLACKBERRY + APPLE + GINGER + LEMON
2. BLACKBERRY + YOGURT + HONEY + BANANA
3. BLACKBERRY + MINT + LEMON + AGAVE NECTAR + WATER

SEASON

Peak during the summer

FLAVOR

Sweet with slight hints of tartness

PROCESSING

Works best in smoothies, can also be used lightly in juices and combined with other ingredients to alter color and impart slight berry flavor to finished juice

CONTAINS

Vitamin C, Vitamin K, Copper, Manganese

A B C D E F G H I J K L M N O P Q R S T U V W X Y Z

Blueberry

SUB CATEGORY: **FRUIT, BERRY**

IN SEASON
AVAILABLE
LIMITED AVAILABILITY

HEALTH BENEFITS

Prevents Alzheimer's, anti-inflammatory, antioxidant, lowers blood pressure, lowers blood sugar, improves brain health, prevents some forms of cancers, improves cardiovascular system, lowers cholesterol, cognitive benefits, prevents diabetes, improves eyesight, strengthens nervous system, prevents neurodegenerative diseases

FLAVOR PAIRING

Agave Nectar
Almond
Apple
Apricot
Banana
Blackberry
Cinnamon
Cucumber
Fennel
Ginger
Honey
Lavender
Lemon
Lime
Mango
Maple Syrup
Melon
Mint
Nectarine
Nutmeg
Orange
Pineapple
Raspberry
Strawberry
Thyme
Vanilla
Watermelon
Yogurt

IDEAS

1. **BLUEBERRY + MINT + YOGURT + HONEY**
2. **BLUEBERRY + THYME + AGAVE NECTAR + LIME + WATER**
3. **BLUEBERRY + LAVENDER + MAPLE SYRUP + STRAWBERRY + YOGURT**

SEASON

Peak spring through summer

FLAVOR

Sweet with slight hints of tartness

PROCESSING

Works best in smoothies, can also be used lightly in juices and combined with other ingredients to alter color and impart slight berry flavor to finished juice

CONTAINS

Vitamin C, Vitamin K, Copper, Manganese

Bok Choy

SUB CATEGORY: **VEGETABLE**

— IN SEASON
— AVAILABLE
— LIMITED AVAILABILITY

HEALTH BENEFITS

Antioxidant, anti-inflammatory, increases cardiovascular system, prevents some forms of cancer, improves bone strength, strengthens heart

FLAVOR PAIRING

Agave Nectar
Apples
Bell Peppers
Broccoli
Burdock Root
Cabbage
Carrots
Celery
Chili Pepper
Cilantro
Garlic
Ginger
Greens
Lettuces
Lemon
Lime
Turmeric

IDEAS

1. BOK CHOY + BEET + RED APPLE + GINGER + LEMON
2. BOK CHOY + CABBAGE + KALE + CUCUMBER + GREEN APPLE + LIME
3. BOK CHOY + CUCUMBER + CELERY + BURDOCK ROOT + CILANTRO + LIME

SEASON

Peak spring through summer

FLAVOR

Bitter and sweet with notes of cabbage and spinach

PROCESSING

Works well in green juices giving unique flavor

CONTAINS

Vitamin A, Vitamin C, Calcium, Vitamin K, Potassium, Vitamin B9-Folate, Vitamin B6, Manganese, Iron

Broccoli

IN SEASON
AVAILABLE
LIMITED AVAILABILITY

SUB CATEGORY: VEGETABLE

HEALTH BENEFITS

Anti-inflammatory, antioxidant, improves bone strength, prevents some forms of cancer, improves cardiovascular system, detoxification, improves eyesight, improves immune system, promotes healthy skin

FLAVOR PAIRING

Almond
Arugula
Basil
Beet
Bell pepper
Cabbage
Carrot
Chili Pepper
Cilantro
Cucumber
Fennel
Garlic
Ginger
Greens
Lemon
Lettuce
Lime
Mint
Parsley
Pear
Snap Pea
Turmeric
Watercress

IDEAS

1. **BROCCOLI + SPINACH + CUCUMBER + ORANGE + GREEN APPLE + LIME**
2. **BROCCOLI + TOMATO + GREEN BELL PEPPER + GARLIC + CELERY + SALT**
3. **BROCCOLI + GREEN BELL PEPPER + CUCUMBER + KALE + LEMON + GINGER**

SEASON

Peak from autumn through winter

FLAVOR

Crisp, light taste with earthy notes and slightly peppery

PROCESSING

When juiced gives a little more peppery taste than green cabbage and slightly less savory

CONTAINS

Vitamin C, Vitamin K, Vitamin B9-Folate, Vitamin A, Manganese

Burdock Root

SUB CATEGORY: VEGETABLE, ROOT

IN SEASON
AVAILABLE
LIMITED AVAILABILITY

HEALTH BENEFITS

Improves immune system, promotes healthy skin, prevents some forms of cancer, prevents gout

SEASON

Peak through summer

FLAVOR

Sweet earthy flavor with slight hints of artichokes

PROCESSING

Great for juicing, as well as pickling

CONTAINS

Vitamin B6, Iron, Manganese

FLAVOR PAIRING

Apples	Lemon
Cabbage	Lettuce
Carrot	Lime
Celery	Nuts
Coconut	Parsnip
Dates	Spinach
Fennel	Tomato
Garlic	
Ginger	
Kale	

IDEAS

1. BURDOCK ROOT + CARROT + LIME + GINGER
2. BURDOCK ROOT + RED APPLE + FENNEL + LEMON
3. BURDOCK ROOT + SWEET POTATO + GREEN APPLE + GINGER + LEMON

Cabbage, Green

SUB CATEGORY: VEGETABLE, LETTUCE

IN SEASON
AVAILABLE
LIMITED AVAILABILITY

HEALTH BENEFITS

Prevents anemia, anti-inflammatory, antioxidant, prevents blood clotting, prevents some forms of cancer, improves cardiovascular system, lowers cholesterol, detoxification, improves immune system, prevents ulcers, improves digestive system

FLAVOR PAIRING

Apple
Bell Pepper
Carrot
Celery
Celery Root
Cilantro
Cucumber
Fennel
Garlic
Ginger
Greens
Horseradish
Lemon
Lettuce
Lime
Parsley
Radish
Tomato

IDEAS

1. GREEN CABBAGE + RED APPLE + FENNEL + LEMON
2. GREEN CABBAGE + GINGER + GREEN APPLE + LIME
3. GREEN CABBAGE + TOMATO + LIME + CELERY + GARLIC + SALT

SEASON

Year-round

FLAVOR

Slightly sweet earthy taste with strong savory notes when juiced

PROCESSING

The juice from cabbages can sometimes be overpowering, It is recommended to combine with stronger flavored items to balance flavor or use sparingly.

CONTAINS

Vitamin K, Vitamin C

Recipe

CANTALOUPE PEAR

INGREDIENTS

CANTALOUPE 73.8%
1lb 1oz / 502g

BOSC PEAR 17.4%
4.2oz / 119g

LEMON 8.2%
2oz / 57g

VANILLA 0.6%
0.15oz / 4g

BENEFITS

1. *Hydrating*
2. *Antioxidant rich*
3. *Lowers cholesterol*

RECIPE YIELD

16 oz / 473 ml

FLAVOR PROFILE

SWEET — SAVORY

LIGHT — BOLD

FRUIT — VEGGIE

Cabbage, Napa

IN SEASON
AVAILABLE
LIMITED AVAILABILITY

SUB CATEGORY: VEGETABLE, LETTUCE

HEALTH BENEFITS

Prevents anemia, anti-inflammatory, antioxidant, prevents blood clotting, prevents some forms of cancer, improves cardiovascular system, lowers cholesterol, detoxification, improves immune system, prevents ulcers, improves digestive system

FLAVOR PAIRING

Almond
Arugula
Basil
Beet
Bell Pepper
Cabbage
Carrot
Chili Pepper
Cilantro
Cucumbers
Fennel
Garlic
Ginger
Greens
Lemon
Lettuce
Lime
Mint
Parsley
Pears
Snap Pea
Turmeric
Watercress

IDEAS

1. NAPA CABBAGE + BEET + CUCUMBER + GINGER + LEMON
2. NAPA CABBAGE + BELL PEPPER + CUCUMBER + KALE + LIME + GINGER
3. NAPA CABBAGE + GREEN APPLE + CILANTRO + CUCUMBER + JALAPEÑO + LIME

SEASON

Year-round

FLAVOR

Crisp light taste with earthy notes and slightly peppery

PROCESSING

When juiced gives a little more peppery taste than green cabbage and slightly less savory

CONTAINS

Vitamin K, Vitamin C, Vitamin B6, Manganese, Potassium

Cabbage, Red

SUB CATEGORY: VEGETABLE, LETTUCE

— IN SEASON
— AVAILABLE
— LIMITED AVAILABILITY

HEALTH BENEFITS

Prevents anemia, anti-inflammatory, antioxidant, prevents blood clotting, prevents some forms of cancer, improves cardiovascular system, lowers cholesterol, detoxification, improves immune system, prevents ulcers, improves digestive system

FLAVOR PAIRING

Apple
Bell Pepper
Carrot
Celery
Celery Root
Cilantro
Cucumber
Fennel
Garlic
Ginger
Greens
Horseradish
Lemon
Lettuce
Lime
Orange
Parsley
Radish
Tomato

IDEAS

1. RED CABBAGE + PINEAPPLE + LEMON + GINGER
2. RED CABBAGE + GRAPE + LIME + GINGER + CUCUMBER
3. RED CABBAGE + CARROT + RED APPLE + GINGER + LEMON

SEASON

Peak autumn through winter

FLAVOR

Slightly sweet earthy taste with strong savory notes when juiced

PROCESSING

Give unique color in small amounts to any juice

CONTAINS

Vitamin K, Vitamin C, Vitamin B6, Vitamin A

A B C D E F G H I J K L M N O P Q R S T U V W X Y Z

Cacao Powder

IN SEASON
AVAILABLE
LIMITED AVAILABILITY

SUB CATEGORY: ADDITIVE

HEALTH BENEFITS

Prevents Alzheimer's disease, anti-depressant, improves cardiovascular system, balances hormones, lowers blood pressure, increases energy, improves metabolism, prevents some forms of cancer, promotes healthy skin, strengthens teeth

FLAVOR PAIRING

Agave Nectar	Coconut	Mint
Almond	Coffee	Nuts
Apple	Date	Orange
Apricot	Dried Fig	Passion Fruit
Banana	Ginger	Pear
Cashew	Goji Berry	Raisin
Cherry	Honey	Raspberry
Chilies	Lemon	Strawberry
Cinnamon	Macadamia Nut	Vanilla
Clove	Maple Syrup	Yogurt

IDEAS

1. CACAO POWDER + ALMOND + WATER + VANILLA + DATE
2. CACAO POWDER + BANANA + YOGURT + HONEY + PEANUT BUTTER
3. CACAO POWDER + MINT + BANANA + HONEY + YOGURT + DARK CHOCOLATE

SEASON

Year-round

FLAVOR

Bitter with light notes of chocolate

PROCESSING

Often mixed in nut mylks and used in smoothies for deep chocolate flavor without the sweetness

CONTAINS

Magnesium, Manganese, Iron, Potassium, Zinc, Copper

Cantaloupe

SUB CATEGORY: **FRUIT, MELON**

IN SEASON
AVAILABLE
LIMITED AVAILABILITY

HEALTH BENEFITS

Anti-coagulant, anti-inflammatory, antioxidant, prevents arteriosclerosis, lowers blood pressure, prevents some forms of cancer, prevents cataracts, lowers cholesterol, prevents diabetes, prevents heart disease, improves immune system, helps promote healthy pregnancy, promotes skin health, relieves stress, improves hydration

FLAVOR PAIRING

Agave Nectar	Ginger	Nutmeg
Basil	Honey	Papaya
Berries	Lemongrass	Peach
Chili Pepper	Lettuce	Raisin
Cilantro	Mango	Vanilla
Cinnamon	Maple Syrup	Yogurt
Citrus	Melon	
Cucumber	Mint	
Date	Nectarine	
Fig	Nuts	

IDEAS

1. CANTALOUPE + GINGER + LEMON
2. CANTALOUPE + BASIL + CUCUMBER + LIME + HONEY
3. CANTALOUPE + CILANTRO + SERRANO CHILI PEPPER + AGAVE NECTAR

SEASON

Peak through summer

FLAVOR

Sweet fresh taste with floral notes

PROCESSING

Flavor pairing both juices and smoothies, there are many varieties available, ranging from mild to sweet with different floral qualities as well, recommended to switch varieties through the season for the sweetest available.

CONTAINS

Vitamin A, Vitamin C, Potassium

Caraway Seed

IN SEASON
AVAILABLE
LIMITED AVAILABILITY

SUB CATEGORY: SPICE, SEED

HEALTH BENEFITS

Lowers cholesterol, prevents some forms of cancer, helps with digestion, antioxidant

FLAVOR PAIRING

Almond
Apple
Cabbage
Carrot
Chili Pepper
Cucumber
Juniper Berry
Lemon
Nutmeg
Orange
Parsley
Pumpkin
Squash
Sweet Potato
Vanilla

IDEAS

1. CARAWAY SEED + CARROTS + RED APPLE + LEMON
2. CARAWAY SEED + ORANGE + FENNEL + CUCUMBER
3. CARAWAY SEED + TOMATO + LEMON + CUCUMBER + SALT + KALE

SEASON

Year -round

FLAVOR

Aromatic spice with notes of dill, licorice, cumin and anise

PROCESSING

Recommend toasting until fragrant to release oils then grinding

CONTAINS

Vitamin C, Iron, Copper

Cardamom

SUB CATEGORY: **SPICE, SEED**

— IN SEASON
— AVAILABLE
— LIMITED AVAILABILITY

HEALTH BENEFITS

Helps with digestion, lowers cholesterol, prevents some forms of cancer, improves cardiovascular health, anti-depressant

FLAVOR PAIRING

Almond
Apple
Cabbage
Carrot
Chili Pepper
Chocolate
Cilantro
Cinnamon
Clove
Coconut
Dates
Ginger
Honey
Lemon
Mango
Maple Syrup
Mint
Orange
Parsley
Pear
Pistachio
Quince
Rose Water
Sweet Potato
Turmeric
Vanilla
Yogurt

IDEAS

1. CARDAMOM + MANGO + HONEY + YOGURT + ROSE WATER
2. CARDAMOM + WATER + DATE + VANILLA + STAR ANISE + HONEY
3. CARDAMOM + CARROT + SWEET POTATO + CINNAMON + LEMON

SEASON

Year-round

FLAVOR

Aromatic spice, slightly sweet with strong spicy notes of flowers, eucalyptus and mint

PROCESSING

Recommend toasting until fragrant to release oils then grinding

CONTAINS

Vitamin A, Vitamin C, Manganese, Copper

Carrot

SUB CATEGORY: **VEGETABLE, ROOT**

IN SEASON
AVAILABLE
LIMITED AVAILABILITY

HEALTH BENEFITS

Prevents acidosis, prevents acne, prevents anemia, anti-inflammatory, antioxidant, prevents atherosclerosis, prevents asthma, prevents some forms of cancer, prevents cataracts, lowers cholesterol, helps with congestion, prevents emphysema, improves immune system, helps promote healthy pregnancy, promotes healthy skin, improves vision, prevents ulcers, improves hydration

FLAVOR PAIRING

Allspice	Cabbage	Coconut	Lettuce	Raisin
Almond	Caraway Seed	Cucumber	Lime	Snap Pea
Apple	Cardamom	Daikon	Maple Syrup	Spinach
Apricot	Cashew	Dates	Mint	Tarragon
Avocado	Celery	Dill	Nutmeg	Tomato
Basil	Chili Pepper	Fennel	Nuts	Turmeric
Beet	Cilantro	Ginger	Orange	Vanilla
Bell Pepper	Cinnamon	Greens	Parsley	Watercress
Broccoli	Citrus	Honey	Parsnip	Yogurt
Burdock	Clove	Lemon	Pineapple	

IDEAS

1. CARROT + APPLE + GINGER + LEMON
2. CARROT + ORANGE + PINEAPPLE + GINGER
3. CARROT + CILANTRO + JALAPENO + LIME + APPLE

SEASON

Peak from summer through autumn

FLAVOR

Sweet aromatic earthy flavor

PROCESSING

A good substitute for pure orange juice is a mixture of 50% carrots and 50% pineapples (taste will be very similar to pure orange juice!), when juicing do not peel only remove the tough to clean knobs at the top end of the carrot.

CONTAINS

Vitamin A, Vitamin K, Vitamin C, Potassium

Cashew

SUB CATEGORY: **NUT**

IN SEASON
AVAILABLE
LIMITED AVAILABILITY

HEALTH BENEFITS

Increases energy, strengthens bones, promotes healthy heart, improves cardiovascular system, antioxidant, promotes weight loss

FLAVOR PAIRING

Almond
Apricot
Banana
Berries
Cardamom
Cayenne
Cilantro
Cinnamon
Clove
Coconut
Ginger
Honey
Lemon
Lime
Mango
Nutmeg
Orange
Pineapple
Pumpkin
Snow Pea
Spinach
Snap Pea
Vanilla
Yogurt

IDEAS

1. CASHEW + CINNAMON + WATER + HONEY
2. CASHEW + MANGO + CARDAMOM + HONEY + YOGURT
3. CASHEW + WATER + DATE + CACAO POWDER + WATER + ALMOND + VANILLA

SEASON

Year-round

FLAVOR

Sweet creamy texture with hints of butter

PROCESSING

When producing nut mylks do not over process or soak more than four hours, the fat will emulsify and make it difficult to extract the mylk, you can toast the cashews slightly before soaking to add a slight caramel toasted flavor, great in smoothies due to their high fat content which lends a smooth texture.

CONTAINS

Magnesium, Phosphorous, Copper, Iron, Protein

Cauliflower

SUB CATEGORY: VEGETABLE

IN SEASON
AVAILABLE
LIMITED AVAILABILITY

HEALTH BENEFITS

Anti-inflammatory, antioxidant, prevents some forms of cancer, improves cardiovascular health, prevents Crohn's disease, detoxification, improves digestion, prevents diabetes, promotes weight loss, prevents arthritis, prevents ulcerative colitis

FLAVOR PAIRING

Almond
Apple
Basil
Bell Pepper
Bok Choy
Broccoli
Cardamom
Carrot
Cashew
Cayenne
Celery
Chili Pepper
Cilantro
Cinnamon
Citrus
Coconut
Ginger
Honey
Horseradish
Kale
Lemon
Lime
Mango
Marjoram
Mint
Nutmeg
Nuts
Orange
Pistachio
Pomegranate
Pumpkin
Snap Pea
Spinach
Squash
Tomato
Turmeric
Watercress
Yogurt

IDEAS

1. **CAULIFLOWER + ORANGE + GINGER**
2. **CAULIFLOWER + RED APPLE + SPINACH + POMEGRANATE + GINGER**
3. **CAULIFLOWER + CELERY + BEET + TOMATO + CUCUMBER + GINGER + SALT**

SEASON

Peak from autumn through winter

FLAVOR

Semi sweet with pungent notes of butter and slight hints of mustard

PROCESSING

When juicing use entire head of cauliflower as well as stems

CONTAINS

Vitamin C, Vitamin K, Vitamin B9-Folate, Choline, Vitamin B6

- IN SEASON
- AVAILABLE
- LIMITED AVAILABILITY

Celery

SUB CATEGORY: VEGETABLE

SEASON
Year-round

FLAVOR
Sweet earthy flavor with slight hints of artichokes

PROCESSING
Great for juicing, as well as pickling

CONTAINS
Vitamin K

HEALTH BENEFITS

Reduces acidity, anti-inflammatory, antioxidant, prevents asthma, lowers blood pressure, prevents some forms of cancer, lowers cholesterol, improves kidney function, improves nervous system, prevents osteoarthritis, prevents rheumatoid arthritis, prevents tumor growth, prevents urinary stones, promotes weight loss

FLAVOR PAIRING

Apple
Basil
Beet
Bell Pepper
Cabbage
Carrots
Cauliflower
Celery Root
Cucumber
Fennel
Garlic
Ginger
Grape
Greens
Kohlrabi
Lemon
Lettuce
Lime
Nuts
Parsley
Pear
Pineapple
Snow Pea
Squash
Tomato
Turmeric
Watercress
Yogurt

IDEAS

1. CELERY + GRAPE + APPLE + LEMON
2. CELERY + KALE + CUCUMBER + GREEN APPLE + LEMON + GINGER
3. CELERY + TOMATO + CUCUMBER + GARLIC + SPINACH + LIME + JALAPEÑO + SALT

Recipe

CARROT REFRESHER

INGREDIENTS

CARROT 61.2%
1lb 10 oz / 501 g

GREEN APPLE 17.8%
5.1 oz / 145 g

RED APPLE 17.8%
5.1 oz / 145 g

LEMON 1.6%
.47 oz / 13 g

GINGER 1.6%
.47 oz / 13 g

BENEFITS

1. *Digestion booster*
2. *Improves vision*
3. *Lowers cholesterol*

RECIPE YIELD

16 oz / 473 ml

FLAVOR PROFILE

SWEET — SAVORY

LIGHT — BOLD

FRUIT — VEGGIE

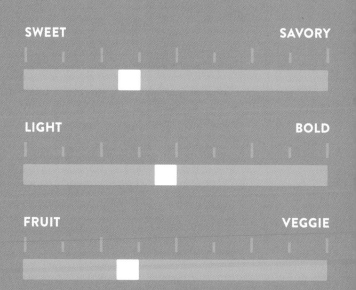

Celery Root

SUB CATEGORY: **VEGETABLE, ROOT**

— IN SEASON
— AVAILABLE
— LIMITED AVAILABILITY

HEALTH BENEFITS

Antioxidant, prevents some forms of cancer, prevents Alzheimer's disease, improves digestion, improves eyesight, anti-inflammatory

FLAVOR PAIRING

Apple	Fennel	Parsley
Beet	Honey	Parsnip
Bell Pepper	Kale	Pear
Cabbage	Kohlrabi	Tomato
Caraway Seed	Lemon	Watercress
Carrot	Lettuce	
Cayenne	Lime	
Celery	Mint	
Celery Seed	Nutmeg	
Chard	Orange	

IDEAS

1. CELERY ROOT + RED APPLE + PEAR + LEMON
2. CELERY ROOT + CARROT + APPLE + LEMON + GINGER
3. CELERY ROOT + KALE + LEMON + GINGER + CUCUMBER + GREEN

SEASON

Autumn through spring

FLAVOR

Earthy flavor with notes of celery, anise and parsley

PROCESSING

Adds a deep earthy flavor to juice

CONTAINS

Vitamin C, Vitamin K, Vitamin B6

A B C D E F G H I J K L M N O P Q R S T U V W X Y Z

Charcoal, Activated

SUB CATEGORY: ADDITIVE

IN SEASON
AVAILABLE
LIMITED AVAILABILITY

HEALTH BENEFITS

Improves digestion, strengthens teeth, detoxification, promotes skin health, lowers cholesterol, anti-aging

FLAVOR PAIRING

Due to its neutral flavor, can be incorporated in almost all juices

IDEAS

1. CHARCOAL + WATER + LEMON + HONEY
2. CHARCOAL + GINGER + LEMON + RED APPLE
3. CHARCOAL + STRAWBERRY + GRAPE + COCONUT WATER + CINNAMON

SEASON

Year-round

FLAVOR

Gritty and strong notes of minerals

PROCESSING

Use sparingly and make sure is labeled Food Grade, believed to remove toxins, be sure to use plastic or wooden spoon and avoid metal, possible to pick up toxins from the utensil

CONTAINS

Not a significant source of vitamins or minerals

Chard, Swiss

SUB CATEGORY: **VEGETABLE, LETTUCE**

IN SEASON
AVAILABLE
LIMITED AVAILABILITY

HEALTH BENEFITS

Anti-inflammatory, antioxidant, strengthens bones, improves cardiovascular system, prevents some forms of cancer, improves brain function, lowers blood pressure, strengthens heart, improves eyesight, prevents osteoarthritis

FLAVOR PAIRING

Apple
Basil
Beet
Bell Pepper
Carrot
Chili Pepper
Cilantro
Cinnamon
Cucumber
Fennel
Garlic
Ginger
Greens
Kale
Lemon
Lettuce
Lime
Mint
Nettle
Orange
Parsley
Tomato

IDEAS

1. CHARD + BEET + CARROT + ORANGE + CUCUMBER
2. CHARD + TOMATO + CUCUMBER + KALE + LEMON + GINGER + GARLIC
3. CHARD + FENNEL + KALE + LIME + GINGER + CUCUMBER + GREEN APPLE

SEASON

Late summer into autumn

FLAVOR

Slightly earthier than spinach and the stalks have a hint of celery taste

PROCESSING

When juicing try to use white stem variety, when you juice the rainbow chard it will sometimes change the juice color to brown

CONTAINS

Vitamin A, Vitamin K, Vitamin C, Magnesium, Copper, Manganese, Potassium, Vitamin E, Iron, Vitamin B2, Calcium

Cherry

IN SEASON
AVAILABLE
LIMITED AVAILABILITY

SUB CATEGORY: FRUIT

HEALTH BENEFITS

Antioxidant, prevents some forms of cancer, anti-inflammatory, sleep-aid, promotes weight-loss, strengthens muscles, prevents osteoarthritis, strengthens heart, lowers blood pressure

FLAVOR PAIRING

Agave Nectar
Allspice
Almond
Apricot
Basil
Blackberry
Cardamom
Cacao Powder
Chili Pepper
Cinnamon
Citrus
Clove
Coconut
Ginger
Honey
Lemon
Mint
Nectarine
Nutmeg
Nuts
Orange
Peach
Pear
Pistachio
Plum
Star Anise
Vanilla
Yogurt

IDEAS

1. CHERRY + YOGURT + VANILLA + HONEY
2. CHERRY + MINT + LEMON + GINGER + PEAR
3. CHERRY + PINEAPPLE + COCONUT + GRAPE + MANGO

SEASON

Summer

FLAVOR

Sweet and slightly tart depending on the variety

PROCESSING

Great for both smoothies and juice when pitted, the sour variety are more nutrient dense

CONTAINS

Vitamin A, Vitamin C

Chia Seeds

SUB CATEGORY: **SEED**

HEALTH BENEFITS

Increase energy, helps aid digestive health, lowers cholesterol level

FLAVOR PAIRING

Due to its neutral flavor, can be incorporated in almost all juices

SEASON

Year-round

FLAVOR

Notes of nuts and poppy seeds

PROCESSING

Can be added to any liquid, after sitting the tiny seeds will soften slightly and form a light gel around its exterior, great way to add texture to juices, vital component to certain mixtures to use as a natural vegetarian thickener for products such as chia puddings

CONTAINS

Fatty acid, Protein, Calcium, Dietary Fiber, Magnesium

IDEAS

1. CHIA SEED + PINEAPPLE + MINT
2. CHIA SEED + COCONUT WATER + CUCUMBER + LIME
3. CHIA SEED + STRAWBERRY + LEMON + ORANGE + HONEY + WATER

Chili Pepper

IN SEASON
AVAILABLE
LIMITED AVAILABILITY

SUB CATEGORY: VEGETABLE

HEALTH BENEFITS

Antioxidant, improves cardiovascular health, improves immune system, prevents Alzheimer's disease, improves eyesight, helps aid digestion

FLAVOR PAIRING

Agave Nectar
Avocado
Basil
Bell Pepper
Cilantro
Cinnamon
Cacao Powder
Coconut
Cucumber
Garlic
Ginger
Honey
Lemon
Lime
Mango
Parsley
Pineapple
Tomato
Turmeric
Yogurt

IDEAS

1. JALAPEÑO CHILI PEPPER + WATERMELON + MINT + LIME
2. JALAPEÑO CHILI PEPPER + MANGO + AGAVE NECTAR + YOGURT + CINNAMON
3. SERRANO CHILI PEPPER + TOMATO + CUCUMBER + CELERY + KALE + LEMON + GINGER + SALT

SEASON

Summer through autumn

FLAVOR

Ranges depending on variety from sweet to spicy

PROCESSING

For the spicy varieties you are able to mellow the spiciness by removing the seeds and white ribs on the inside before juicing

CONTAINS

Vitamin C, Vitamin B6-pholate, Vitamin K, Vitamin A, Manganese

Cilantro

SUB CATEGORY: **HERB**

— IN SEASON
— AVAILABLE
— LIMITED AVAILABILITY

HEALTH BENEFITS

Lowers cholesterol, antioxidant, promotes skin health, prevents some forms of cancer, strengthens bones, prevents Alzheimer's disease

FLAVOR PAIRING

Avocado
Basil
Beet
Bell Pepper
Cardamom
Celery
Chard
Chili Pepper
Cinnamon
Citrus
Coconut
Cucumber
Ginger
Greens
Jicama
Lemon
Lime
Mango
Mint
Orange
Parsley
Pear
Pineapple
Squash
Sweet Potato
Tomato
Yogurt

IDEAS

1. CILANTRO + KALE + CUCUMBER + GREENS
2. CILANTRO + PINEAPPLE + JALAPEÑO + CUCUMBER
3. CILANTRO + KALE + CUCUMBER + GREEN APPLE + GINGER + LIME

SEASON

Year-round, peaking spring through summer

FLAVOR

Slightly sweet with pungent notes of lemon/ lime and parsley

PROCESSING

When juicing or blending use both leaves and stem

CONTAINS

Vitamin A, Vitamin C, Vitamin K

Cinnamon

— IN SEASON
— AVAILABLE
— LIMITED AVAILABILITY

SUB CATEGORY: SPICE

HEALTH BENEFITS

Strengthens muscles, improves immune system, antioxidant, anti-inflammatory, strengthens heart, lowers blood-sugar, helps with blood pressure, anti-viral qualities, prevents Alzheimer's disease, prevents Parkinson's disease, prevents some forms of cancer

FLAVOR PAIRING

Agave Nectar
Almond
Apple
Banana
Beet
Blueberry
Carrot
Chili Pepper
Cacao Powder
Clove
Coconut
Coffee
Date
Ginger
Grapefruit
Grape
Honey
Lemon
Maple Syrup
Nutmeg
Nuts
Orange
Peach
Pear
Raisin
Rose Water
Sweet Potato
Vanilla
Yogurt

IDEAS

1. CINNAMON + MANGO + YOGURT + LIME
2. CINNAMON + APPLE + LEMON + GINGER + NUTMEG + CLOVE
3. CINNAMON + SWEET POTATO + RED APPLE + GINGER + LEMON

SEASON

Year-round

FLAVOR

Bitter, slightly sweet and very aromatic

PROCESSING

Ceylon variety is slightly sweeter, lighter and milder than the more common cassia variety, as well as containing different nutrients

CONTAINS

Vitamin C, Calcium, Iron

Coconut, Meat

SUB CATEGORY: **TREE FRUIT**

— IN SEASON
— AVAILABLE
— LIMITED AVAILABILITY

HEALTH BENEFITS

Strengthens muscles, improves immune system, antioxidant, anti-inflammatory, strengthens heart, lowers blood sugar, prevents Alzheimer's diesease, prevents Parkinsons disease, prevents some forms of cancer

FLAVOR PAIRING

Agave Nectar	Coconut	Nuts
Almond	Coffee	Orange
Apple	Date	Peach
Banana	Ginger	Pear
Beet	Grapefruit	Raisin
Blueberry	Grape	Rose Water
Carrots	Honey	Sweet Potato
Chili Pepper	Lemon	Vanilla
Cacao Powder	Maple Syrup	Yogurt
Clove	Nutmeg	

IDEAS

1. COCONUT MEAT + COCONUT WATER
2. COCONUT MEAT + PINEAPPLE + MINT + LIME
3. COCONUT MEAT + CHERRY + MANGO + PINEAPPLE + ORANGE + YOGURT

SEASON

Year-round

FLAVOR

Slightly sweet with savory undertones

PROCESSING

Can be blended smooth with coconut water to produce coconut mylk, can be left slightly chunky and added to juice to give some texture and infuse the coconut flavor, due to its high fat content will emulsify well in smoothie applications

CONTAINS

Vitamin B6-Folate, Vitamin C, Magnesium, Manganese, Iron, Potassium

Coconut, Oil

IN SEASON
AVAILABLE
LIMITED AVAILABILITY

SUB CATEGORY: OIL

HEALTH BENEFITS

Strengthens muscles, improves immune system, antioxidant, anti-inflammatory, strengthens heart, lowers blood sugar, prevents Alzheimer's disease, prevents Parkinson's disease, prevents some forms of cancer

FLAVOR PAIRING

Agave Nectar	Date	Mint
Almond	Ginger	Nuts
Apricot	Grapefruit	Orange
Banana	Honey	Pomegranate
Carrot	Kaffir Lime Leaf	Raspberry
Cherry	Kiwi	Strawberry
Chili Pepper	Lemon	Sweet Potato
Chocolate	Lime	Turmeric
Cinnamon	Maple Syrup	Vanilla
Cranberry	Melon	Yogurt

IDEAS

1. COCONUT OIL + ALMOND MYLK
2. COCONUT OIL + PINEAPPLE + ORANGE + LIME
3. COCONUT OIL + YOGURT + COCONUT MYLK + HONEY + VANILLA

SEASON

Year-round

FLAVOR

Mild coconut flavor

PROCESSING

Coconut oil can be added to smoothies and nut mylks to give them a richer taste, a trick to incorporate evenly is to slightly warm the oil before adding, also when adding to nut mylks be sure to shake well right before serving to break up the oil when it congeals from the cool temps

CONTAINS

Fat and saturated fat

Recipe

COCONUT NUT MYLK

INGREDIENTS

COCONUT WATER 76.6%
15.7 oz / 445 g

ALMONDS 15.6%
3.2 oz / 91 g

MACADAMIA NUT 5.9%
1.2 oz / 34 g

VANILLA EXTRACT 0.6%
.12 oz / 3 g

DATES 0.6%
.12 oz / 3 g

PINK SALT 0.4%
.08 oz / 2 g

COCONUT EXTRACT 0.4%
.08 oz / 2 g

BENEFITS

1. *Hydrating*
2. *Improves muscle healing/health*
3. *Lowers blood pressure*

RECIPE YIELD

16 oz / 473 ml

FLAVOR PROFILE

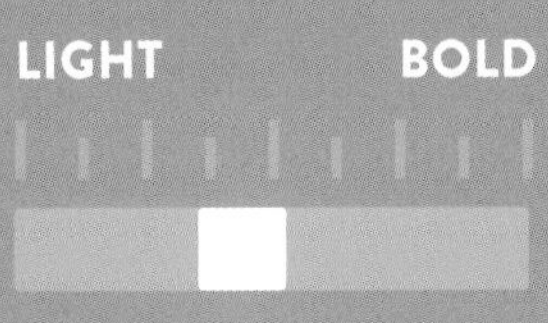

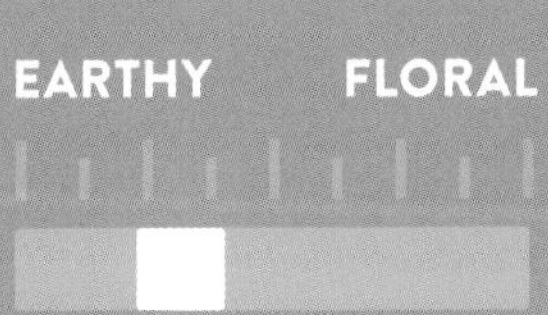

Coconut, Water

— IN SEASON
— AVAILABLE
— LIMITED AVAILABILITY

SUB CATEGORY: **TREE-FRUIT**

HEALTH BENEFITS

Antioxidant rich, promotes weight loss, promotes healthy hair

FLAVOR PAIRING

Agave Nectar
Almond
Apricot
Banana
Carrot
Cherry
Chili Pepper
Chocolate
Cinnamon
Cranberry
Date
Ginger
Grapefruit
Honey
Kaffir Lime Leaf
Kiwi
Lemon
Lime
Maple Syrup
Melon
Mint
Nuts
Orange
Pomegranate
Raspberry
Strawberry
Sweet Potato
Turmeric
Vanilla
Yogurt

IDEAS

1. COCONUT WATER + LIME
2. COCONUT WATER + ALMOND + HONEY + VANILLA + SALT
3. COCONUT WATER + MANGO + KAFFIR LIME LEAF + AGAVE NECTAR

SEASON

Year-round

FLAVOR

Semi sweet with notes of nuts

PROCESSING

Can be used as a base for juice or blended into a smoothie

CONTAINS

Not a significant source of vitamins or minerals

Cranberry

SUB CATEGORY: **FRUIT, BERRY**

— IN SEASON
— AVAILABLE
— LIMITED AVAILABILITY

HEALTH BENEFITS

Prevents anemia, anti-aging, antioxidant, anti-inflammatory, prevents atherosclerosis, prevents some forms of cancer, improves cardiovascular system, lowers cholesterol, improves immune system, improves eyesight, prevents kidney stones, probiotic, promotes healthy skin, prevents stomach ulcers, prevents venous disorders, prevents urinary tract infections

FLAVOR PAIRING

Agave Nectar
Allspice
Apple
Apricot
Beet
Chili Pepper
Cinnamon
Clove
Date
Fig
Ginger
Honey
Jicama
Nutmeg
Nuts
Orange
Pear
Pomegranate
Pumpkin
Raspberry
Squash
Sweet Potato
Vanilla
Watermelon
Yogurt

IDEAS

1. CRANBERRY + WATERMELON + LIME + MINT
2. CRANBERRY + APPLE + ORANGE + GINGER
3. CRANBERRY + POMEGRANATE + PEAR + LEMON

SEASON

Autumn through winter

FLAVOR

Tart, slightly bitter and sour

PROCESSING

Flavor pairing sweeter fruit will bring out the natural flavor from the cranberries to balance out the tartness

CONTAINS

Vitamin C, Manganese

Cucumber

IN SEASON
AVAILABLE
LIMITED AVAILABILITY

SUB CATEGORY: **VEGETABLE**

HEALTH BENEFITS

Prevents acid reflux, anti-inflammatory, antioxidant, prevents arthritis, improves cardiovascular system, prevents asthma, lowers blood pressure, prevents some forms of cancer, prevents diabetes, prevents gout, promotes healthy skin

FLAVOR PAIRING

Apple
Apricot
Arugula
Avocado
Basil
Beet
Bell Pepper
Cabbage
Carrots
Cayenne
Celery
Chili Pepper
Cilantro
Citrus
Fennel
Garlic
Ginger
Grape
Greens
Hibiscus
Honey
Horseradish
Jicama
Kale
Lemon
Lettuce
Lime
Mango
Melon
Mint
Orange
Papaya
Parsley
Peach
Pear
Pineapple
Plum
Pomegranate
Spinach
Strawberry
Tarragon
Tomato
Turmeric
Watercress
Watermelon
Yogurt

IDEAS

1. CUCUMBER + LEMON + MINT + HONEY
2. CUCUMBER + BEET + ORANGE + GINGER
3. CUCUMBER + HONEYDEW + GINGER + LIME

SEASON

Year-round, peaking from spring through summer

FLAVOR

Mild refreshing neutral flavor with hints of melon

PROCESSING

Great vegetable to use in juicing to tone down sharp flavors, peel skin to not affect the juice color

CONTAINS

Vitamin K

Cumin

SUB CATEGORY: **SPICE**

HEALTH BENEFITS

Improves digestion, prevents diabetes, improves cardiovascular system, strengthens immune system, prevents insomnia, prevents anemia, improves lactation for nursing mothers, prevents some forms of cancer

FLAVOR PAIRING

Avocado
Bell Pepper
Cabbage
Carrot
Chili Pepper
Cilantro
Cinnamon
Clove
Garlic
Ginger
Lemon
Lime
Root Vegetables
Tamarind
Tomato
Turmeric
Yogurt

IDEAS

1. CUMIN + CARROT + LEMON
2. CUMIN + GINGER + LEMON + TURMERIC
3. CUMIN + TOMATO + CARROT + BELL PEPPER + GARLIC + LEMON

SEASON

Autumn through winter

FLAVOR

Pungent earthy nutty spicy taste with hints of lemon

PROCESSING

Toasting the seeds before grinding will release the oils and make the spice more fragrant and flavorful, tends to work with mostly savory blends

CONTAINS

Iron, Magnesium, Calcium, Phosphorus, Vitamin B1

Daikon

IN SEASON
AVAILABLE
LIMITED AVAILABILITY

SUB CATEGORY: **VEGETABLE, ROOT**

HEALTH BENEFITS

Improves cardiovascular system, natural detoxifier, improves immune system, improves digestion system, prevents some forms of cancer, anti-inflammatory, strengthens bones, promotes weight loss, promotes healthy skin

FLAVOR PAIRING

Agave Nectar
Apple
Bell Pepper
Bok Choy
Cabbage
Carrot
Cilantro
Cucumber
Garlic
Ginger
Greens
Honey
Lemon
Lime
Pear
Radish
Scallion
Snow Pea
Wasabi

IDEAS

1. DAIKON + GREEN APPLE + LIME + CUCUMBER
2. DAIKON + KALE + CELERY + GREEN APPLE + LEMON + GINGER
3. DAIKON + CARROT + SWEET POTATO + CINNAMON + RED APPLE

SEASON

Autumn through winter

FLAVOR

Slightly bitter and sweet with hints of radishes

PROCESSING

Can be used in place of of pepper or slightly spicy component to blends, add a crisp radish note to juices

CONTAINS

Vitamin C, Vitamin B6, Folate, Potassium, Copper

Date

IN SEASON
AVAILABLE
LIMITED AVAILABILITY

SUB CATEGORY: TREE FRUIT

HEALTH BENEFITS

Aids in digestion, prevents some forms of cancer, increases energy, strengthens bones, improves immune system, promotes weight loss, prevents risk of stroke, improves eyesight, improves nervous system

FLAVOR PAIRING

Almond
Apple
Apricot
Banana
Carrot
Cherry
Chocolate
Cinnamon
Clove
Coffee
Coconut
Flaxseed
Ginger
Honey
Lemon
Maple Syrup
Nutmeg
Nuts
Orange
Pear
Pumpkin
Rice
Vanilla
Yogurt

IDEAS

1. DATE + ALMOND MYLK + MATCHA
2. DATE + ALMOND MYLK + CACAO NIBS
3. DATE + COFFEE + ALMOND MYLK + VANILLA

SEASON

Year-round

FLAVOR

Sweet deep flavor with notes of caramel

PROCESSING

Most commonly used as sweet element in nut mylks and smoothies, lends a deep sweet flavor when incorporated

CONTAINS

Magnesium, Copper, Potassium

A B C D E F G H I J K L M N O P Q R S T U V W X Y Z

Dill

— IN SEASON
— AVAILABLE
— LIMITED AVAILABILITY

SUB CATEGORY: HERB

HEALTH BENEFITS

Aids in digestion, prevents insomnia, strengthens bones, prevents gas, prevents diabetes, prevents arthritis, anti-inflammatory, improves respiratory system

FLAVOR PAIRING

Asparagus
Basil
Beet
Bell Pepper
Cabbage
Caraway Seed
Carrot
Celery
Chive
Cilantro
Cucumber
Fennel
Garlic
Ginger
Greens
Honey
Horseradish
Kale
Kohlrabi
Lemon
Orange
Spinach
Tomato
Yogurt

IDEAS

1. DILL + CARROT + GINGER + ORANGE
2. DILL + TOMATO + CARROT + LEMON + GARLIC + CUCUMBER
3. DILL + CUCUMBER + BEET + FENNEL + CILANTRO + GINGER + LEMON

SEASON

Year-round

FLAVOR

Notes of caraway and anise, strong distinct flavor when juiced

PROCESSING

When juicing, do not discard the stems, most of the flavor is in the stems

CONTAINS

Not a significant source of vitamins or minerals

Echinacea

SUB CATEGORY: OIL

IN SEASON
AVAILABLE
LIMITED AVAILABILITY

HEALTH BENEFITS

Prevents some forms of cancer, strengthens immune system, wound healing qualities, strengthens bones and teeth, anti-inflammatory, promotes respiratory health

FLAVOR PAIRING

Due to its neutral flavor, can be incorporated in almost all juices

IDEAS

1. ECHINACEA OIL + GINGER + APPLE + CAYENNE
2. ECHINACEA OIL + ORANGE + LEMON + GINGER
3. ECHINACEA OIL + LIME + LEMON + ORANGE + HONEY

SEASON

Year-round

FLAVOR

Neutral flavor

PROCESSING

Echinacea is an herb most commonly found in either oil or extract form, believed to help fight infections and boost immune system, most commonly added to ginger for cold fighting shots

CONTAINS

Not a significant source of vitamins or minerals

Fennel *(Anise)*

IN SEASON
AVAILABLE
LIMITED AVAILABILITY

SUB CATEGORY: **VEGETABLE, ROOT**

HEALTH BENEFITS

Anti-inflammatory, antioxidant, strengthens immune system, prevents some forms of cancer, strengthens cardiovascular health, lowers cholesterol, lowers blood pressure

FLAVOR PAIRING

Arugula
Asparagus
Avocado
Basil
Beet
Bell Pepper
Carrot
Celery
Chard
Chili Pepper
Citrus
Coriander
Cucumber
Fig
Ginger
Greens
Honey
Lemon
Lime
Mango
Mint
Nuts
Peach
Pear
Pomegranate
Radish
Snap Pea
Star Anise
Tomato
Vanilla

IDEAS

1. FENNEL + BEET + GINGER + LEMON
2. FENNEL + ORANGE + PEACH + MINT
3. FENNEL + TOMATO + CELERY + GARLIC

SEASON

Year-round, peaking from autumn through winter

FLAVOR

Sweet and fresh flavor with hints of anise and licorice

PROCESSING

Trim only bottom base and use entire vegetable, the fronds from the top are lighter and more delicate in flavor

CONTAINS

Vitamin C, Potassium, Manganese

Fig, Dried

SUB CATEGORY: **FRUIT, DRIED**

IN SEASON
AVAILABLE
LIMITED AVAILABILITY

HEALTH BENEFITS

Lowers blood pressure, promotes weight loss, strengthens cardiovascular system, strengthens heart, prevents some forms of cancer, strengthens bones, prevents macular degeneration

FLAVOR PAIRING

Almond
Anise Seed
Apple
Banana
Berries
Cardamom
Cinnamon
Coconut
Cranberry
Dates
Honey
Lemon
Orange
Pear
Pistachio
Raisin
Yogurt

IDEAS

1. DRIED FIG + BERRIES + YOGURT + HONEY
2. DRIED FIG + ALMOND MYLK + CINNAMON + CARDAMOM
3. DRIED FIG + ALMOND MYLK + PISTACHIO + HONEY + ROSE WATER

SEASON

Year-round

FLAVOR

Sweet with subtle notes of honey, raisins and nuts

PROCESSING

Since being dry, they work best when soaked in a liquid before processing, works well as sweet element in nut mylks

CONTAINS

Not a significant source of vitamins or minerals

A B C D E F G H I J K L M N O P Q R S T U V W X Y Z

Fig, Fresh

IN SEASON
AVAILABLE
LIMITED AVAILABILITY

SUB CATEGORY: FRUIT

HEALTH BENEFITS

Lowers blood pressure, promotes weight loss, strengthens cardiovascular system, strengthens heart, prevents some forms of cancer, strengthens bones, prevents macular degeneration

FLAVOR PAIRING

Anise seed
Apple
Berries
Cardamom
Chili Pepper
Cinnamon
Clove
Coconut
Fennel
Ginger
Grape
Honey
Lavender
Lemon
Lime
Melon
Mint
Molasses
Nuts
Orange
Peach
Persimmon
Pomegranate
Thyme
Vanilla
Yogurt

IDEAS

1. FRESH FIG + YOGURT + HONEY + LAVENDER
2. FRESH FIG + LIME + YOGURT + MINT + HONEY
3. FRESH FIG + STRAWBERRY + VANILLA + ALMOND MYLK

SEASON

Summer through autumn

FLAVOR

Slightly sweet deep berry flavor with hints of hazelnuts

PROCESSING

Fresh figs do not contain that much juice which makes them great for blending into smoothies

CONTAINS

Not a significant source of vitamins or minerals

Flaxseed

SUB CATEGORY: ADDITIVE

HEALTH BENEFITS

Best source for omega-3, antioxidant, anti-inflammatory, prevents some forms of cancer, aids in digestion, prevents hypertension, strengthens liver, prevents depression, lowers cholesterol

FLAVOR PAIRING

Apple
Avocado
Banana
Carrot
Citrus
Coriander
Fennel
Grain
Honey
Kale
Nuts
Yogurt

IDEAS

1. FLAXSEED + FENNEL + ORANGE + PEAR
2. FLAXSEED + YOGURT + HONEY + BANANA + PEANUT BUTTER
3. FLAXSEED + CORIANDER + COCONUT WATER + LIME + CARROT

IN SEASON
AVAILABLE
LIMITED AVAILABILITY

SEASON

Year-round

FLAVOR

Slight nutty flavor with hints of wheat and grass

PROCESSING

Flaxseeds are high in fiber and omega-3 fatty acids, flaxseeds can either be ground and processed the same as nut mylks or ground directly into smoothies

CONTAINS

Omega-3 fats, Vitamin B1, Copper, Manganese, Magnesium, Phosphorus

Recipe

HEALTHY GREEN

INGREDIENTS

KALE 29.2%
7 oz / 201 g

CUCUMBER 29.2%
7 oz / 201 g

GREEN APPLE 24.3%
5.9 oz / 167 g

CELERY 9.8%
2.4 oz / 67 g

LEMON 4.9%
1.2 oz / 33 g

GINGER 2.6%
.62 oz / 18 g

BENEFITS

1. *Antioxidant rich*
2. *Skin purifying*
3. *Reduces cholesterol*

RECIPE YIELD

16 oz / 473 ml

FLAVOR PROFILE

SWEET — SAVORY

LIGHT — BOLD

FRUIT — VEGGIE

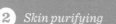

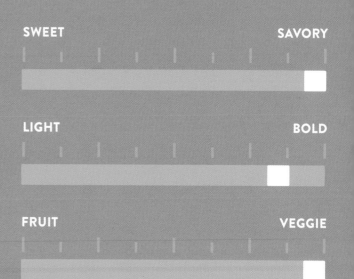

Garlic

SUB CATEGORY: VEGETABLE

IN SEASON
AVAILABLE
LIMITED AVAILABILITY

HEALTH BENEFITS

Antibiotic, anti-coagulant, anti-inflammatory, prevents atherosclerosis, lowers blood pressure, prevents some forms of cancer, improves cardiovascular health, lowers cholesterol, stengthens immune system, prevents fungal infection, prevents heart disease, promotes weight loss, prevents peptic ulcer, improves respiratory system

FLAVOR PAIRING

Asparagus
Basil
Beet
Broccoli
Carrot
Chard
Chili Pepper
Fennel
Greens
Kale
Lemon
Lettuce
Spinach
Tomatillo
Tomato
Turmeric

IDEAS

1. GARLIC + TOMATILLO + CHARD + LIME + CARROT
2. GARLIC + TOMATO + CELERY + KALE + CARROT
3. GARLIC + KALE + CELERY + LIME + SPINACH + GINGER

SEASON

Year -round

FLAVOR

Slightly sweet with pungent notes of onion

PROCESSING

Use in moderation with savory blends to add a depth of flavor

CONTAINS

Manganese, Vitamin B6, Vitamin C

A B C D E F G H I J K L M N O P Q R S T U V W X Y Z

Ginger

SUB CATEGORY: **VEGETABLE, ROOT**

IN SEASON
AVAILABLE
LIMITED AVAILABILITY

HEALTH BENEFITS

Reduces pain, anti-inflammation, improves cardiovascular system, prevents ulcers, aids in digestion, improves immune system

FLAVOR PAIRING

Almond
Apple
Apricot
Asparagus
Banana
Basil
Bell Pepper
Berries
Bok Choy
Broccoli
Burdock
Cardamom
Carrot
Celery
Chili Pepper
Cilantro
Cinnamon
Coconut
Fennel
Fig
Grapefruit
Greens
Honey
Jicama
Lemon
Lime
Mango
Maple Syrup
Mint
Orange
Papaya
Parsley
Passion Fruit
Peach
Pear
Pineapple
Plum
Pumpkin
Rhubarb
Spinach
Sweet Potato
Tomato
Turmeric
Yogurt

IDEAS

1. GINGER + BEET + LEMON + PEAR
2. GINGER + LEMON + WATER + CAYENNE + MAPLE SYRUP
3. GINGER + PINEAPPLE + JALAPEÑO + MINT + JICAMA + CILANTRO

SEASON

Year-round, peaking summer through winter

FLAVOR

Spicy pungent notes of both citrus and pepper

PROCESSING

One of the key elements in juicing, it adds depth and balances the flavor, always cut the ginger then smell when using, the flavor can range in strength depending on how long ago and what season it was harvested

CONTAINS

Vitamin B6, Magnesium, Manganese

Goji Berry, Dried

SUB CATEGORY: **FRUIT, DRIED**

IN SEASON
AVAILABLE
LIMITED AVAILABILITY

HEALTH BENEFITS

Improves immune system, increses mental function, increases cardiovascular health, promotes weight loss, natural sleep aid, prevents diabetes, lowers blood pressure

FLAVOR PAIRING

Almond
Banana
Berries
Chocolate
Coconut
Date
Ginger
Lemon
Lime
Orange
Pear
Pomegranate
Raspberry
Sweet Potato
Yogurt

IDEAS

1. GOJI BERRY + ALMOND + DATE + FIVE SPICE
2. GOJI BERRY + ACAI + YOGURT + HONEY + CINNAMON
3. GOJI BERRY + FIG + STRAWBERRY + ALMOND MYLK + BASIL + HONEY

SEASON

Year-round

FLAVOR

Slightly sweet with hints of tart dried cherries and dried cranberries

PROCESSING

Can be added to finished juice to infuse flavor, also can be blended into nut mylk and smoothies

CONTAINS

Amino acids, Antioxidants, Vitamin A

A B C D E F G H I J K L M N O P Q R S T U V W X Y Z

Grapefruit

IN SEASON
AVAILABLE
LIMITED AVAILABILITY

SUB CATEGORY: CITRUS

HEALTH BENEFITS

Anti-inflammatory, antioxidant, prevents asthma, prevents arthritis, prevents some forms of cancer, improves cardiovascular health, lowers cholesterol, strengthens immune system, prevents diabetes, improves digestive health, increases energy, prevents heart attack, prevents insomnia, prevents kidney stones, prevents arthritis, prevents sore throat, reduces risk of stroke, prevents tumors, promotes weight loss

FLAVOR PAIRING

Agave Nectar	Greens	Orange
Arugula	Honey	Passionfruit
Avocado	Jicama	Pear
Chili Pepper	Kale	Pineapple
Cilantro	Kiwi	Pomegranate
Cinnamon	Lemon	Rosemary
Citrus	Lime	Strawberry
Coconut	Maple Syrup	Tarragon
Fennel	Melon	Vanilla
Ginger	Mint	Yogurt

IDEAS

1. GRAPEFRUIT + ORANGE + LIME + MINT
2. GRAPEFRUIT + CANTALOUPE + PEAR + MINT
3. GRAPEFRUIT + POMEGRANATE + CUCUMBER

SEASON

Year-round, peaking through winter

FLAVOR

Tart, tangy and slightly bitter

PROCESSING

Grapefruits typically have a thick pith, when being juiced it is best if it is peeled first

CONTAINS

Vitamin C, Vitamin A

Grape

SUB CATEGORY: **FRUIT**

— IN SEASON
— AVAILABLE
— LIMITED AVAILABILITY

HEALTH BENEFITS

Anti-acne, anti-aging, anti-inflammation, antioxidant, atherosclerosis, bladder health, lowers blood pressure, lowers blood sugar, cancer preventative, cardiovascular health, lowers cholesterol, cognitive, eye health, immune system, heart disease, kidney health, liver health, migrane/headache, nervous system, respiratory health, skin health

FLAVOR PAIRING

Apple	Fig	Mint	Watermelon
Arugula	Ginger	Nutmeg	Yogurt
Banana	Grapefruit	Nuts	
Basil	Greens	Orange	
Blueberry	Honey	Pear	
Carrot	Jicama	Rosemary	
Cinnamon	Lemon	Star Anise	
Clove	Lime	Strawberry	
Cucumber	Mango	Vanilla	
Fennel	Melon	Watercress	

IDEAS

1. GREEN GRAPE + PINEAPPLE + MINT + CUCUMBER
2. BLACK GRAPE + BEET + PEAR + LEMON + GINGER
3. RED GRAPE + STRAWBERRY + COCONUT WATER + CINNAMON

SEASON

Year-round, peaking summer through autumn

FLAVOR

Black and red varieties refreshingly sweet with hints of berry, green variety slightly crisper

PROCESSING

When choosing which variety of grape to use, it is best to pair based off of color of produce being used, similar color produce will pair better with similar color grapes

CONTAINS

Vitamin K, Vitamin C, Copper

Greens, Collard

SUB CATEGORY: **VEGETABLE, LETTUCE**

HEALTH BENEFITS

Anti-inflammatory, antioxidant, prevents atherosclerosis, promotes blood health, increases bone strength, prevents some forms of cancer, strengthens cardiovascular system, prevents cataracts, lowers cholesterol, detoxification, prevents diabetes, improves eyesight, prevents heart disease, improves immune system, improves lung strength, promotes healthy skin

FLAVOR PAIRING

- Apple
- Avocados
- Basil
- Beet
- Bell Pepper
- Cabbage
- Carrot
- Celery
- Chili Pepper
- Citrus
- Cucumber
- Fennel
- Garlic
- Greens
- Ginger
- Kale
- Lemon
- Lime
- Orange
- Sweet Potato
- Tomato
- Turmeric

IDEAS

1. COLLARD GREENS + GREEN APPLE + PINEAPPLE + CUCUMBER
2. COLLARD GREENS + CARROT + TOMATO + BELL PEPPER + GARLIC + LIME
3. COLLARD GREENS + CUCUMBER + CELERY + GINGER + GREEN APPLE + LEMON

SEASON

Year-round, peaking autumn through spring

FLAVOR

Bitter and slightly sweet with notes of pepper

PROCESSING

When juicing greens do not remove the stem, collards like most leafy greens, are loaded with vitamins and nutrients

CONTAINS

Vitamin K, Vitamin A, Vitamin C, Vitamin B9-Folate, Manganese, Calcium, Tryptophan, Choline, Iron, Vitamin B6, Vitamin B2- riboflavin, Magnesium

Greens, Dandelion

SUB CATEGORY: **VEGETABLE, LETTUCE**

— IN SEASON
— AVAILABLE
— LIMITED AVAILABILITY

HEALTH BENEFITS

Lowers blood pressure, prevents some forms of cancer, strengthens bones, reduces stress, antioxidant, aids in digestion, prevents cataracts, promotes healthy skin

FLAVOR PAIRING

Apple
Avocado
Basil
Beet
Bell Pepper
Cabbage
Carrot
Celery
Chili Pepper
Citrus
Cucumber
Fennel
Garlic
Greens
Ginger
Kale
Lemon
Lime
Orange
Sweet Potato
Tomato
Turmeric

IDEAS

1. DANDELION GREENS + PINEAPPLE + GREEN APPLE + CUCUMBER
2. DANDELION GREENS + CUCUMBER + BEET + ORANGE + GINGER
3. DANDELION GREENS + CELERY + LEMON + GINGER + CUCUMBER + GREEN APPLE

SEASON

Year-round

FLAVOR

Bitter and slightly sour with pungent notes of pepper

PROCESSING

When juicing do not remove the stem, the dandelion greens have a strong flavor, works well when paired with cucumber to mellow flavor and combines other strong flavored items as well

CONTAINS

Vitamin A, Vitamin C, Vitamin K, Calcium

Greens, Turnip

IN SEASON
AVAILABLE
LIMITED AVAILABILITY

SUB CATEGORY: **VEGETABLE, LETTUCE**

HEALTH BENEFITS

Anti-inflammatory, antioxidant, atherosclerosis, prevents cancer, improves cardiovascular health, lowers cholesterol, detoxification, promotes heart health, strengthens immune system, reverses rheumatoid arthritis

FLAVOR PAIRING

Apple
Avocado
Basil
Beet
Bell Pepper
Cabbage
Carrot
Celery
Chili Pepper
Citrus
Cucumber
Fennel
Garlic
Greens
Ginger
Kale
Lemon
Lime
Orange
Sweet Potato
Tomato
Turmeric

IDEAS

1. TURNIP GREENS + CUCUMBER + ORANGE + FENNEL
2. TURNIP GREENS + TOMATO + CELERY + CARROT + GARLIC + LEMON
3. TURNIP GREENS + PINEAPPLE + BASIL + CUCUMBER + LIME + GINGER

SEASON

Year-round

FLAVOR

Slightly bitter with notes of mustard greens

PROCESSING

Juice leafy part along with the stem, the stem will have a slightly stronger mustard green flavor than the leaf

CONTAINS

Vitamin K, Vitamin A, Vitamin C, Manganese, Vitamin E, Iron, Copper, Magnesium, Potassium

Guava

SUB CATEGORY: **FRUIT**

— IN SEASON
— AVAILABLE
— LIMITED AVAILABILITY

HEALTH BENEFITS

Promotes weight loss, improves eyesight, prevents diabetes, improves digestion system, prevents some forms of cancer, improves immune system, promotes healthy skin

FLAVOR PAIRING

Apple
Banana
Cashew
Chocolate
Cinnamon
Citrus
Coconut
Ginger
Honey
Lemon
Lime
Mango
Nutmeg
Nuts
Orange
Papaya
Pear
Pineapple
Plum
Quince
Strawberries
Vanilla
Yogurt

IDEAS

1. GUAVA + BANANA + MANGO + YOGURT
2. GUAVA + COCONUT MYLK + STRAWBERRY + VANILLA
3. GUAVA + MANGO + YOGURT + ORANGE + LIME + MINT

SEASON

Year-round, peaking summer through autumn

FLAVOR

Sweet and slightly sour with light floral notes

PROCESSING

Due to the guavas texture it is best to blend lightly with water, do not over blend or the seeds will give a gritty taste to the finished juice, after blending it is best when strained

CONTAINS

Vitamin C, Potassium, Vitamin B9-Folate, Copper, Manganese

Hazelnut

IN SEASON
AVAILABLE
LIMITED AVAILABILITY

SUB CATEGORY: NUT

HEALTH BENEFITS

Anti-aging, helps produce blood cells, prevents some forms of cancer, strengthens cardiovascular system, lowers cholesterol, prevents urinary tract infections

FLAVOR PAIRING

Almond	Fig	Pineapple
Apple	Grape	Raisin
Apricot	Honey	Raspberry
Banana	Maple Syrup	Rhubarb
Berries	Mint	Sweet Potato
Cherry	Nutmeg	Vanilla
Chocolate	Orange	
Cinnamon	Passion Fruit	
Coffee	Peach	
Cranberry	Pear	

IDEAS

1. HAZELNUT + COCONUT MYLK + COFFEE + MINT
2. HAZELNUT + ALMOND MYLK + CINNAMON + NUTMEG
3. HAZELNUT + ALMOND MYLK + CACAO POWDER + HONEY

SEASON

Year-round

FLAVOR

Slightly sweet with hints of butter, coconut and cream

PROCESSING

If you roast right before processing it will bring through a stronger, deeper and richer flavor

CONTAINS

Magnesium, Copper, Vitamin E, Manganese, Iron, Calcium, Vitamin C, Vitamin B6, Folate

Recipe

HONEYDEW YUZU

INGREDIENTS

HONEYDEW 89.7%
1 lb 3 oz / 544 g

GREEN APPLE 5.8%
1.2 oz / 35 g

YUZU JUICE 3.7%
.80 oz / 23 g

KAFFIR LIME LEAF 0.7%
.16 oz / 5 g

BENEFITS

1. *Hydrating*
2. *Immunity booster*

RECIPE YIELD

16 oz / 473 ml

FLAVOR PROFILE

SWEET — SAVORY

LIGHT — BOLD

FRUIT — VEGGIE

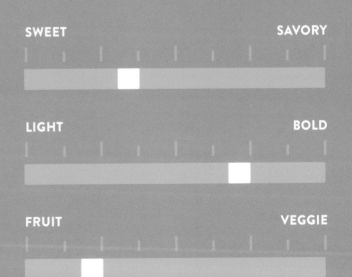

Hemp, Seed

IN SEASON
AVAILABLE
LIMITED AVAILABILITY

SUB CATEGORY: ADDITIVE

HEALTH BENEFITS

Prevents arthritis, promotes weight loss, strengthens hair, skin and nails, increases digestive health, prevents some forms of cancer, strengthens heart

FLAVOR PAIRING

Apple
Avocado
Beet
Bell Pepper
Carrot
Chili Pepper
Cilantro
Citrus
Cucumber
Fennel
Garlic
Ginger
Grapefruit
Greens
Horseradish
Jicama
Lemon
Lime
Mint
Orange
Parsley
Peach
Pear
Pineapple
Pomegranate
Raspberry
Snap Pea
Strawberry
Tangerine
Tomato

IDEAS

1. HEMP SEED + ALMOND MYLK + MANGO + DATE
2. HEMP SEED + YOGURT + HONEY + PEANUT BUTTER + CACAO
3. HEMP SEED + STRAWBERRY + ALMOND MYLK + BANANA + MINT

SEASON

Year-round

FLAVOR

Nutty flavor with hints of sunflower seeds, walnuts and pine nuts

PROCESSING

Hemp seeds are high in omega-3 fatty acids, can be either ground or blended into smoothies or even processed the same way as you would a nut mylk

CONTAINS

Iron, Magnesium, Zinc

Honey

SUB CATEGORY: SWEETENER

— IN SEASON
— AVAILABLE
— LIMITED AVAILABILITY

HEALTH BENEFITS

Strengthens immune system, increases energy, increases memory, promotes sleep, antioxidant

FLAVOR PAIRING

Apple	Ginger	Pear
Apricot	Grapefruit	Peanut Butter
Banana	Hazelnut	Plum
Cardamom	Lavender	Quince
Chocolate	Lemon	Raisin
Cinnamon	Lime	Raspberry
Citrus	Melon	Rhubarb
Clove	Mint	Seeds
Coconut	Nutmeg	Vanilla
Fig	Orange	Yogurt

IDEAS

1. HONEY + ALMOND MYLK + VANILLA
2. HONEY + YOGURT + CACAO NIBS + MINT + BANANA
3. HONEY + PEANUT BUTTER + ALMOND MYLK + BANANA

SEASON

Year-round

FLAVOR

Sweet, syrupy flavor with slight deep hints from floral to caramel

PROCESSING

Great for uses in smoothies and almond mylks, the deeper the honey color the deeper the flavor, always try to use local when possible to assist with allergies

CONTAINS

Not a significant source of vitamins or minerals

A B C D E F G H I J K L M N O P Q R S T U V W X Y Z

Honey, Manuka

SUB CATEGORY: **SWEETENER**

IN SEASON
AVAILABLE
LIMITED AVAILABILITY

HEALTH BENEFITS

Wound healing, helps with stomach ulcers, soothes heartburn

FLAVOR PAIRING

Apple	Ginger	Pear
Apricot	Grapefruit	Peanut Butter
Banana	Hazelnut	Plum
Cardamom	Lavender	Quince
Chocolate	Lemon	Raisin
Cinnamon	Lime	Raspberry
Citrus	Melons	Rhubarb
Clove	Mint	Seeds
Coconut	Nutmeg	Vanilla
Fig	Orange	Yogurt

IDEAS

1. HONEY + GRAPEFRUIT + FENNEL + MINT
2. HONEY + LIME + GINGER + COCONUT WATER
3. HONEY + LAVENDER + ALMOND MYLK + CASHEW

SEASON

Year-round

FLAVOR

Sweet, syrupy flavor with slight deep hints from floral to caramel

PROCESSING

Manuka honey, if produced in New Zealand, contains high levels of enzymes thanks to the manuka bush used to pollinate, is added to juices, smoothies and mylks for its antibacterial and antiviral qualities

CONTAINS

Enzymes, Hydrogen peroxide, Proteins

Honeydew

SUB CATEGORY: **FRUIT, MELON**

IN SEASON
AVAILABLE
LIMITED AVAILABILITY

HEALTH BENEFITS

Lowers blood pressure, prevents dehydration, aids in digestion, improves immune system, strengthens teeth and bones, improves eyesight, promotes healthy skin, promotes weight loss

FLAVOR PAIRING

Arugula
Basil
Berries
Cayenne
Cinnamon
Cucumbers
Ginger
Honey
Kiwi
Lemon
Lime
Maple Syrup
Melons
Mint
Papaya
Pepper
Pomegranate
Vanilla
Yogurt

IDEAS

1. HONEYDEW + LIME + CUCUMBER
2. HONEYDEW + GINGER + ARUGULA + LIME + GRAPEFRUIT
3. HONEYDEW + POMEGRANATE + CUCUMBER + VANILLA

SEASON

Year-round, peaking late spring through summer

FLAVOR

Sweet, crisp taste with slight floral notes

PROCESSING

Great for using for hydration properties

CONTAINS

Vitamin C

Horseradish

IN SEASON
AVAILABLE
LIMITED AVAILABILITY

SUB CATEGORY: VEGETABLE, ROOT

HEALTH BENEFITS

Strengthens heart, strengthens cardiovascular system, improves immune system, prevents some forms of cancer, prevents arthritis, aids in weight loss, increases energy, strengthens digestion

FLAVOR PAIRING

Apple
Arugula
Avocado
Beet
Cabbage
Carrot
Celery
Cucumber
Garlic
Greens
Lemon
Lime
Parsley
Pepper
Root Vegetables
Rosemary
Sage
Sorrel
Tomatillo
Tomato
Watercress

IDEAS

1. HORSERADISH + TOMATO + GARLIC + BELL PEPPER + CELERY + CUCUMBER
2. HORSERADISH + KALE + LEMON + GREEN APPLE + GINGER + CELERY + CUCUMBER
3. HORSERADISH + CARROT + LEMON + TOMATILLO + GINGER + SPINACH + CUCUMBER

SEASON

Year-round, peaking from late fall through spring

FLAVOR

Strong, pungent, bitter, peppery taste with notes of mustard

PROCESSING

Flavor pairing with savory blends adds a slight heat and peppery notes to juices

CONTAINS

Vitamin C

Jicama

SUB CATEGORY: VEGETABLE, ROOT

— IN SEASON
— AVAILABLE
— LIMITED AVAILABILITY

HEALTH BENEFITS

Improves digestion, strengthens immune system, strengthens cardiovascular system, lowers blood pressure, strengthens bones, promotes weight loss

FLAVOR PAIRING

Apple
Arugula
Basil
Beet
Bell Pepper
Berries
Broccoli
Carrot
Cayenne
Chili Pepper
Cilantro
Citrus
Cucumber
Ginger
Grapefruit
Horseradish
Lemon
Lime
Mango
Melon
Mint
Orange
Papaya
Pear
Pineapple
Spinach
Tomato
Watercress
Watermelon

IDEAS

1. JICAMA + CUCUMBER + PEAR + MINT
2. JICAMA + PINEAPPLE + JALAPEÑO + CILANTRO
3. JICAMA + GINGER + GRAPEFRUIT + CANTALOUPE

SEASON

Year-round, peaking through autumn

FLAVOR

Slightly sweet and crisp with hints of water chestnuts

PROCESSING

Great when added to stronger flavored ingredients when juicing to mellow out the flavor and add another dimension

CONTAINS

Vitamin C, Iron

A B C D E F G H I J K L M N O P Q R S T U V W X Y Z

Kaffir Lime Leaf

— IN SEASON
— AVAILABLE
— LIMITED AVAILABILITY

SUB CATEGORY: **HERB**

HEALTH BENEFITS

Strengthens oral health, improves digestive system, natural detoxifier, promotes healthy skin, reduces stress, reduces inflammation, strengthens hair

FLAVOR PAIRING

Apple
Arugula
Avocado
Beet
Cabbage
Carrot
Celery
Cucumber
Garlic
Greens
Lemon
Lime
Parsley
Pepper
Root Vegetables
Rosemary
Sage
Sorrel
Tomatillo
Tomato
Watercress

IDEAS

1. KAFFIR LIME LEAF + MANGO + YOGURT + MINT
2. KAFFIR LIME LEAF + COCONUT + PEAR + PINEAPPLE
3. KAFFIR LIME LEAF + CUCUMBER + HONEYDEW + LIME

SEASON

Year-round

FLAVOR

Sour and aromatic notes with herbal citrus tones

PROCESSING

Add sparingly into juices to give herbal lime flavor without the sourness, fresh leaves can be kept frozen to preserve flavor until needed

CONTAINS

Vitamin C

Kale

IN SEASON
AVAILABLE
LIMITED AVAILABILITY

SUB CATEGORY: VEGETABLE, LETTUCE

HEALTH BENEFITS

Helps prevent Alzheimer's disease, anti-inflammatory, antioxidant, blood clotting, blood pressure, prevents cancer, cardiovascular health, prevents cataracts, lowers cholesterol, fights dementia, detoxification, improves digestive health, promotes eye health, maintains heart health, prevents macular degeneration, prevents osteoporosis, promotes healthy skin

FLAVOR PAIRING

Almond	Celery	Orange
Apple	Chard	Oregano
Arugula	Chili Pepper	Parsley
Avocado	Cilantro	Snow Pea
Basil	Garlic	Spinach
Beet	Grapefruit	Sweet Potato
Bell Pepper	Greens	Tomato
Bok Choy	Lemon	Walnut
Cabbage	Mint	
Carrot	Nuts	

IDEAS

1. KALE + BEET + ORANGE + CUCUMBER
2. KALE + PINEAPPLE + GREEN APPLE + MINT
3. KALE + CELERY + LEMON + GINGER + CUCUMBER + GREEN APPLE

SEASON

Year-round, peaking through winter

FLAVOR

Bitter and slightly sweet with light notes of cabbage

PROCESSING

One of the major staples of the juicing world, kale is perfect when added to juice due to its high nutrient and vitamin count, juice the stems and leaves, different varieties will change color of finished juice and intensity of flavor

CONTAINS

Vitamin K, Vitamin A, Vitamin C, Manganese, Copper

A B C D E F G H I J K L M N O P Q R S T U V W X Y Z

Kelp, Powder

IN SEASON
AVAILABLE
LIMITED AVAILABILITY

SUB CATEGORY: ADDITIVE

HEALTH BENEFITS

Anti-inflammatory benefits, helps regulate blood sugar levels, essential for cellular metabolism, promotes cardiovascular health, improves thyroid function, prevents some forms of cancer, lowers cholesterol, improves hydration, promotes weight loss

SEASON

Year-round

FLAVOR PAIRING

Apple
Arugula
Avocado
Basil
Beet
Bell Pepper
Bok Choy
Cabbage
Carrot
Celery
Chard
Chili Pepper
Cilantro
Grapefruit
Greens
Lemon
Lettuce
Mint
Orange
Oregano
Parsley
Pineapple
Snow Pea
Spinach
Sweet Potato
Tomato

FLAVOR

Strong taste of seaweed

PROCESSING

Can typically be used sparingly in green smoothies and green juices

CONTAINS

Calcium, Iodine, B Vitamins

IDEAS

1. KELP POWDER + PINEAPPLE + CUCUMBER
2. KELP POWDER + TOMATO + GARLIC + LEMON + CARROT + CELERY + SALT
3. KELP POWDER + SPINACH + CELERY + CUCUMBER + GREEN APPLE + LEMON + GINGER

Kiwi

SUB CATEGORY: FRUIT

HEALTH BENEFITS

Prevents anemia, anti-inflammatory, antioxidant, prevents asthma, prevents atherosclerosis, blood clotting, balances blood sugar, inhibits skin cancer, promotes cardiovascular health, strengthens immune system, protects from macular degeneration, prevents muscle cramps, relieves mental fatigue, helps prevent osteoarthritis and rheumatoid arthritis, protects against stomach ulcer, reduces risk of stroke, prevents wrinkles

FLAVOR PAIRING

Apple	Ginger	Mint
Avocado	Grapefruit	Orange
Banana	Grape	Papaya
Berries	Greens	Passionfruit
Cherry	Honey	Pineapple
Chocolate	Jicama	Raspberry
Cinnamon	Lemon	Strawberry
Citrus	Lime	Vanilla
Coconut	Mango	Watermelon
Cucumber	Melon	Yogurt

IDEAS

1. KIWI + HONEYDEW + LIME
2. KIWI + GRAPEFRUIT + PINEAPPLE + MINT
3. KIWI + YOGURT + STRAWBERRY + HONEY

IN SEASON
AVAILABLE
LIMITED AVAILABILITY

SEASON

Year-round

FLAVOR

Sweet and sour notes with light hints of berries and melon

PROCESSING

Best to peel the kiwi before processing, if skin is left on the finished product can result in a bitter, slightly off taste, can be used as an ingredient in both juices and smoothies

CONTAINS

Vitamin C, Vitamin K, Vitamin E

Recipe

ROSEMARY LEMONADE

INGREDIENTS

PINEAPPLE 46.1%
14.2 oz / 403 g

ORANGE 44.9%
13.8 oz / 391 g

LEMON 3.5%
1 oz / 30 g

RAW HONEY 3.5%
1 oz / 30 g

ROSEMARY 2.1%
.64 oz / 18 g

BENEFITS

1. *Digestion booster*
2. *Immunity booster*

RECIPE YIELD

16 oz / 473 ml

FLAVOR PROFILE

SWEET — SAVORY

LIGHT — BOLD

FRUIT — VEGGIE

Lavender

SUB CATEGORY: **HERB**

HEALTH BENEFITS

Fights depression, helps with insomnia, prevents headaches, prevents vomiting, prevents some forms of cancer, prevents acne, relieves stress, promotes restful sleep

SEASON

Spring through summer

FLAVOR PAIRING

Apricot
Arugula
Basil
Berries
Cherry
Cinnamon
Citrus
Coconut
Fig
Guava
Honey
Lemon
Mango
Mint
Nectarine
Nuts
Orange
Peach
Plum
Rhubarb
Vanilla
Walnut
Watercress
Yogurt

FLAVOR

Bitter, sour and strong tones of herbs, citrus, flowers

PROCESSING

Can be blended and strained into juices and nut mylks, use sparingly, the flavor is very strong and can become overpowering

CONTAINS

Not a significant source of vitamins or minerals

IDEAS

1. LAVENDER + ALMOND MYLK + HONEY
2. LAVENDER + WATERMELON + CUCUMBER + LIME
3. LAVENDER + STRAWBERRY + YOGURT + HONEY + VANILLA

A B C D E F G H I J K L M N O P Q R S T U V W X Y Z

Lemon

IN SEASON
AVAILABLE
LIMITED AVAILABILITY

SUB CATEGORY: **CITRUS**

HEALTH BENEFITS

Natural antibiotic, anti-inflammatory, antioxidant, prevents asthma, prevents atherosclerosis, prevents some forms of cancer, strengthens immune system, improves digestion, prevents heartburn, promotes heart health, prevents rheumatoid arthritis, promotes healthy skin, prevents stroke

FLAVOR PAIRING

Arugula	Coconut	Lime	Snap Pea
Avocado	Cucumber	Mango	Tomato
Basil	Fennel	Maple Syrup	Vanilla
Beet	Garlic	Mint	
Bell Pepper	Greens	Nuts	
Berries	Ginger	Orange	
Broccoli	Guava	Papaya	
Cardamom	Honey	Parsley	
Carrot	Kale	Peach	
Chocolate	Lavender	Pear	

IDEAS

1. LEMON + WATER + LAVENDER + HONEY
2. LEMON + GINGER + CAYENNE + RED APPLE
3. LEMON + GRAPEFRUIT + ORANGE + GINGER

SEASON
Year-round

FLAVOR
Pungent sourness with light floral notes

PROCESSING
Lemons have a thin skin and pith, the skin is typically left on when processed, adding lemons to juices and smoothies works well to cut through items that are overly sweet and rich in flavor, also helps keep colors vibrant in juices for a longer period of time

CONTAINS
Vitamin C

Lemon, Verbena

SUB CATEGORY: **HERB**

IN SEASON
AVAILABLE
LIMITED AVAILABILITY

HEALTH BENEFITS

Promotes weight loss, strengthens muscles, anti-inflammatory, strengthens immune system, improves digestion, prevents anxiety, regulates appetite

FLAVOR PAIRING

Arugula
Avocado
Basil
Beet
Bell Pepper
Berries
Broccoli
Cardamom
Carrot
Chocolate
Coconut
Cucumber
Fennel
Garlic
Greens
Ginger
Guava
Honey
Kale
Lavender
Lime
Mango
Maple Syrup
Mint
Nuts
Orange
Papaya
Parsley
Peach
Pear
Snap Pea
Tomato
Vanilla

IDEAS

1. LEMON VERBENA + BLUEBERRY + YOGURT + HONEY
2. LEMON VERBENA + GINGER + ORANGE + COCONUT WATER
3. LEMON VERBENA + PEAR + JALAPEÑO + JICAMA + CILANTRO

SEASON

Year-round, peaking during summer

FLAVOR

Similar flavor to lemon without the sour and tart notes, with strong herbal flavor

PROCESSING

Makes a great addition to juices and smoothies when you want to introduce lemon flavor without the tartness, can also be steeped in water to infuse flavor

CONTAINS

Not a significant source of vitamins or minerals

Lettuce (Bibb, Boston, Butter)

IN SEASON
AVAILABLE
LIMITED AVAILABILITY

SUB CATEGORY: **VEGETABLE, LETTUCE**

HEALTH BENEFITS

Prevents some forms of cancer, improves eyesight, increases bone strength, prevents some forms of diabetes, strengthens oral health, lowers cholesterol

FLAVOR PAIRING

Apple
Avocado
Basil
Bell Pepper
Carrot
Celery
Chili Pepper
Cilantro
Cucumber
Fennel
Garlic
Ginger
Grapefruit
Greens
Herbs
Honey
Jicama
Kale
Lemon
Mint
Orange
Parsley
Persimmon
Pomegranate
Snap Pea
Tomato
Yogurt

IDEAS

1. BUTTER LETTUCE + GRAPEFRUIT + MINT + GINGER + HONEY
2. BUTTER LETTUCE + LIME + GINGER + GREEN APPLE + ORANGE
3. BUTTER LETTUCE + TOMATO + BEET + CELERY + LEMON + GINGER

SEASON

Year-round

FLAVOR

Sweet and crisp flavor with slight notes of butter

PROCESSING

Very consistent product typically hydroponically grown, adds light lettuce flavor to juices and blends well into savory style smoothies

CONTAINS

Vitamin A, Vitamin K, Vitamin C

Lettuce, Romaine

SUB CATEGORY: **VEGETABLE, LETTUCE**

SEASON

Year-round

FLAVOR

Sweet with slight bitterness and a crisp, refreshing taste

PROCESSING

One of the most popular variety of greens, can add many nutrients and vitamins when added to juices, important to add a form of citrus or something to lower the pH to keep the green color vibrant

CONTAINS

Vitamin A, Vitamin K, Vitamin C, Vitamin B9-Folate

HEALTH BENEFITS

Anti-anemic, anti-inflammatory, antioxidant, lowers blood pressure, strengthens bones, lowers cholesterol, improves eyesight, improves hydration, strengthens immune system, promotes healthy skin

FLAVOR PAIRING

Apple
Avocado
Basil
Beet
Carrots
Celery
Chili Pepper
Cilantro
Garlic
Ginger
Grapefruit
Greens
Jicama
Lemon
Lime
Mango
Orange
Parsley
Pear
Pomegranate
Sprouts
Tarragon
Tomato
Watercress
Yogurt

IDEAS

1. ROMAINE + GRAPEFRUIT + ORANGE + BASIL + CUCUMBER
2. ROMAINE + PINEAPPLE + MINT + JALAPEÑO + GREEN APPLE
3. ROMAINE + LEMON + GINGER + CUCUMBER + GREEN APPLE

A B C D E F G H I J K L M N O P Q R S T U V W X Y Z

Lime

— IN SEASON
— AVAILABLE
— LIMITED AVAILABILITY

SUB CATEGORY: CITRUS

HEALTH BENEFITS

Natural antibiotic, anti-inflammatory, antioxidant, prevents asthma, prevents atherosclerosis, prevents some forms of cancer, strengthens immune system, improves digestion, prevents heartburn, strengthens heart health, prevents rheumatoid arthritis, promotes healthy skin, prevents stroke

FLAVOR PAIRING

Apple	Chili Pepper	Lemon	Raspberry
Apricot	Cilantro	Lettuce	Tomatoes
Arugula	Coconut	Lychee	Tropical Fruit
Avocado	Cucumber	Mango	Watermelon
Banana	Ginger	Melon	Yogurt
Bell Pepper	Grape	Mint	
Berries	Greens	Orange	
Strawberry	Guava	Papaya	
Broccoli	Honey	Pear	
Carrot	Jicama	Pomegranate	

IDEAS

1. LIME + WATERMELON + MINT
2. LIME + MINT + CUCUMBER + PINEAPPLE
3. LIME + COCONUT WATER + STRAWBERRY

SEASON

Year-round

FLAVOR

Bitter and sour with slight floral notes

PROCESSING

Limes have a thin skin and pith, the skin is typically left on when processed, adding lime to juices and smoothies works well to cut through items that are overly sweet and rich in flavor, also helps keep colors vibrant in juices for a longer period of time

CONTAINS

Vitamin C

Lychee

SUB CATEGORY: FRUIT

IN SEASON
AVAILABLE
LIMITED AVAILABILITY

HEALTH BENEFITS

Lowers risk of some forms of cancer, promotes weight loss, improves cardiovascular strength, strengthens immune system, balances blood pressure, promotes healthy skin, strengthens digestive system

FLAVOR PAIRING

Almond
Berries
Cherry
Chili Pepper
Cilantro
Coconut
Ginger
Grapefruit
Honey
Jicama
Kiwi
Lemon
Lime
Mango
Melon
Mint
Nectarine
Orange
Passion Fruit
Peach
Pear
Pineapple
Plum
Rose Water
Vanilla
Yogurt

IDEAS

1. LYCHEE + CANTALOUPE + LIME
2. LYCHEE + KIWI + PINEAPPLE + MINT
3. LYCHEE + COCONUT WATER + PEAR + GINGER + JALAPEÑO

SEASON

Late spring through summer

FLAVOR

Aromatic and sweet with hints of grapes and cherries

PROCESSING

Need to be deseeded and outer shell peeled off, works best when blended into juices or smoothies for aromatic sweetness

CONTAINS

Vitamin C, Vitamin B6, Copper

A B C D E F G H I J K L M N O P Q R S T U V W X Y Z

Maca, Powder

IN SEASON
AVAILABLE
LIMITED AVAILABILITY

SUB CATEGORY: ADDITIVE

HEALTH BENEFITS

Hormonal function, boosts libido, mental function, increases energy, promotes healthy skin

FLAVOR PAIRING

Agave Nectar
Apple
Apricot
Banana
Berries
Carrot
Cherry
Chocolate
Cacao Nibs
Cinnamon
Coconut
Coffee
Date
Fig
Ginger
Grape
Hazelnut
Honey
Lavender
Maple Syrup
Molasses
Peach
Pear
Pecan
Pistachio
Raisin
Rose Water
Vanilla
Yogurt

IDEAS

1. MACA POWDER + RED GRAPE + STRAWBERRY
2. MACA POWDER + CARROT + RED APPLE + GINGER + LEMON
3. MACA POWDER + ALMOND MYLK + CACAO POWDER + HONEY

SEASON

Year-round

FLAVOR

Earthy, slightly nutty and hints of butterscotch

PROCESSING

Maca powder is believed to balance hormone levels and give a boost of energy, typically found in powder form from the maca root, works well in juices and mylks as well as being blended into smoothies

CONTAINS

Amino acids, Vitamins, Enzymes

Macadamia Nut

SUB CATEGORY: NUT

— IN SEASON
— AVAILABLE
— LIMITED AVAILABILITY

HEALTH BENEFITS

Improves heart health, antioxidant, promotes weight loss, improves bone strength, increases energy, stabilizes blood pressure

SEASON

Year-round

FLAVOR

Slightly sweet with light butter flavor

PROCESSING

Can be used in nut mylks or blended into smoothies, if you toast before processing the flavor will become stronger and add a richness to the drink

CONTAINS

Vitamin B6, Thiamin, Iron, Magnesium, Manganese, Phosphorus, Vitamin B3

FLAVOR PAIRING

Agave Nectar
Apple
Apricot
Banana
Berries
Carrot
Cherry
Chocolate
Cacao Nib
Cinnamon
Coconut
Coffee
Date
Fig
Ginger
Grape
Hazelnut
Honey
Lavender
Maple Syrup
Molasses
Peach
Pear
Pecan
Pistachio
Raisin
Rose Water
Vanilla
Yogurt

IDEAS

1. MACADAMIA NUT + ALMOND MYLK + PEANUT BUTTER + HONEY
2. MACADAMIA NUT + CACAO NIB + ALMOND MYLK + AGAVE NECTAR
3. MACADAMIA NUT + ALMOND MYLK + LAVENDER + VANILLA + MAPLE SYRUP

Mango

IN SEASON
AVAILABLE
LIMITED AVAILABILITY

SUB CATEGORY: **FRUIT**

HEALTH BENEFITS

Prevents some forms of cancer, lowers cholesterol, prevents acne, promotes healthy skin, promotes weight loss, improves eyesight, strengthens digestive system, improves immune system, helps with brain health and memory

FLAVOR PAIRING

Almond
Arugula
Avocado
Banana
Basil
Bell Pepper
Berries
Cardamom
Cashew
Cayenne
Chili Pepper
Cilantro
Cinnamon
Clove
Coconut
Cucumber
Fennel
Ginger
Greens
Honey
Jicama
Kaffir Lime Leaf
Kiwi
Lavender
Lemon
Lime
Melon
Mint
Nuts
Orange
Papaya
Parsley
Passion Fruit
Peach
Pear
Pineapple
Rhubarb
Spinach
Star Anise
Sweet Potato
Tamarind
Tropical Fruit
Vanilla
Yogurt

IDEAS

1. MANGO + YOGURT + CINNAMON + LIME
2. MANGO + PEAR + ORANGE + PASSION FRUIT
3. MANGO + CANTALOUPE + GINGER + CILANTRO + LIME

SEASON

Year-round, peaking spring through summer

FLAVOR

Sweet with light notes of pineapple, honey and peaches

PROCESSING

Due to its texture, the mango does not juice very well but works great blended into smoothies, one way to incorporate into juice is blending with a little liquid and then mixing into juice as a puree

CONTAINS

Vitamin C, Vitamin A, Vitamin B6

BY ARI SEXNER

Recipe

MATCHA ALMOND MYLK

INGREDIENTS

ALKALINE WATER 64.1%
16.2 oz / 459 g

ALMOND 28.3%
7.1 oz / 201 g

HONEY 5.1%
1.3 oz / 37 g

MATCHA POWDER 1.9%
.48 oz / 14 g

VANILLA BEAN 0.6%
.16 oz / 5 g

BENEFITS

1. *Antioxidant rich*
2. *Strengthens heart*
3. *Improves muscle healing / health*

RECIPE YIELD

16 oz / 473 ml

FLAVOR PROFILE

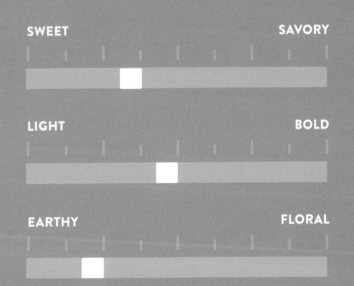

SWEET — SAVORY

LIGHT — BOLD

EARTHY — FLORAL

A B C D E F G H I J K L M N O P Q R S T U V W X Y Z

Maple Syrup

- IN SEASON
- AVAILABLE
- LIMITED AVAILABILITY

SUB CATEGORY: SWEETENER

HEALTH BENEFITS

Anti-inflammatory, antioxidant rich, fights against some forms of cancer, promotes healthy skin, improves digestive system

FLAVOR PAIRING

Allspice	Ginger
Apple	Lemon
Banana	Nutmeg
Berries	Nuts
Cardamom	Orange
Carrot	Peach
Cinnamon	Pear
Citrus	Pumpkin
Clove	Sweet Potato
Fig	Vanilla

IDEAS

1. MAPLE SYRUP + GRAPEFRUIT + PEAR + CAYENNE
2. MAPLE SYRUP + NUT MYLK + PUMPKIN PUREE + VANILLA
3. MAPLE SYRUP + SWEET POTATO + CARROTS + CINNAMON + RED APPLE

SEASON

Year-round

FLAVOR

Sweet with hints of caramel, honey and butter

PROCESSING

Can be added to juices and mylks as a natural sweetener, the darker the grade the deeper the flavor of caramel that comes through

CONTAINS

Magnesium, Potassium, Zinc, Manganese, Copper

Matcha, Powder

IN SEASON
AVAILABLE
LIMITED AVAILABILITY

SUB CATEGORY: **ADDITIVE**

HEALTH BENEFITS

Antioxidant, increases energy, boosts memory, calms nerves, helps with concentration, natural detoxifier, strengthens immune system, lowers cholesterol

FLAVOR PAIRING

Agave Nectar
Almond
Avocado
Banana
Berries
Cacao
Coconut
Coffee
Ginger
Honey
Kale
Lettuce
Mango
Pineapple

SEASON

Year-round

FLAVOR

Slightly sweet, umami flavor

PROCESSING

Found in powder form, Matcha is known as an antioxidant powerhouse, works best when added to smoothies and nut mylks as well as green juices

CONTAINS

Not a significant source of vitamins or minerals

IDEAS

1. MATCHA POWDER + COFFEE + ALMOND MYLK
2. MATCHA POWDER + ALMOND MYLK + CACAO + HONEY
3. MATCHA POWDER + KALE + AVOCADO + YOGURT + PINEAPPLE

A B C D E F G H I J K L M N O P Q R S T U V W X Y Z

Mint

SUB CATEGORY: HERB

— IN SEASON
— AVAILABLE
— LIMITED AVAILABILITY

HEALTH BENEFITS

Improves digestion, prevents nausea, prevents headaches, improves respiratory system, helps with asthma, helps prevent depression, promotes healthy skin, prevents memory loss, promotes weight loss, improves oral health, prevents allergies, prevents some forms of cancer

FLAVOR PAIRING

Almond	Fig	Mango
Apple	Ginger	Melon
Basil	Grapefruit	Orange
Bell Pepper	Grape	Parsley
Carrot	Greens	Peach
Chili Pepper	Jicama	Pear
Chocolate	Kale	Pineapple
Cilantro	Lemon	Spinach
Citrus	Lime	Watermelon
Cucumber	Lychee	Yogurt

IDEAS

1. MINT + PINEAPPLE + GREEN APPLE
2. MINT + WATERMELON + GREEN APPLE
3. MINT + PEAR + JICAMA + CILANTRO + JALAPEÑO

SEASON

Year-round

FLAVOR

Fresh, slightly sweet crisp flavor with pungent herbal notes

PROCESSING

Works well in both smoothies and juices, for juices be sure to include the stem - the stem contains quite a bit of flavor, when added to juices it can either be processed in or added directly into the juice after processing

CONTAINS

Not a significant source of vitamins or minerals

Orange

SUB CATEGORY: **CITRUS**

— IN SEASON
— AVAILABLE
— LIMITED AVAILABILITY

SEASON

Year-round

FLAVOR

Sweet and slightly tart with crisp flavor

PROCESSING

The skin and pith of the orange give a bitter taste to the juice if processed with the flesh, recommended to process while avoiding this part of the orange, throughout the seasons the flavors of different varieties will range from sweet to tart, by changing varieties through the seasons you can get a more consistent flavor

CONTAINS

Vitamin C, Vitamin B9-Folate

HEALTH BENEFITS

Helps prevent Alzheimer's disease, improves immune system, anti-inflammatory, antioxidant, helps prevent asthma, lowers blood pressure, lowers blood sugar, prevents some forms of cancer, improves cardiovascular health, lowers cholesterol, assists against Crohn's disease, helps prevent diabetes, helps with ear infections, prevents gallstones, fights gingivitis, improves heart health, helps against osteoarthritis, helps against Parkinson's disease, helps against rheumatoid arthritis, promotes healthy skin

FLAVOR PAIRING

Apple
Apricot
Arugula
Avocado
Bananas
Basil
Beet
Berries
Broccoli
Cabbage
Cardamom
Carrot
Chili Pepper
Chocolate
Cilantro
Cinnamon
Citrus
Clove
Coconut
Daikon
Date
Fennel
Fig
Ginger
Greens
Honey
Horseradish
Jicama
Kiwi
Mango
Maple Syrup
Mint
Nuts
Papaya
Parsley
Pear
Pepper
Pineapple
Plum
Pomegranate
Snow Pea
Spinach
Star Anise
Star Fruit
Sweet Potatoes
Vanilla
Watercress
Yogurt

IDEAS

1. ORANGE + FENNEL + POMEGRANATE
2. ORANGE + PEAR + CILANTRO + JALAPEÑO
3. ORANGE + GRAPEFRUIT + LEMON + GINGER + HONEY

Oregano, Oil

IN SEASON
AVAILABLE
LIMITED AVAILABILITY

SUB CATEGORY: OIL

HEALTH BENEFITS

Anti-inflammatory, antioxidant rich, strengthens respiratory system, strengthens immune system, prevents viruses, prevents allergies, helps with digestion

FLAVOR PAIRING

Beet
Bell Pepper
Carrot
Cayenne
Celery
Chili Pepper
Citrus
Fennel
Garlic
Ginger
Grapefruit
Honey
Lavender
Lemon
Lime
Orange
Parsley
Pepper, Black
Pineapple
Spinach
Tomato

IDEAS

1. OREGANO OIL + LIME + CAYENNE + GINGER + ORANGE
2. OREGANO OIL + TOMATO + GARLIC + LEMON + CELERY + SALT
3. OREGANO OIL + LEMON + ORANGE + GRAPEFRUIT + APPLE CIDER VINEGAR

SEASON

Year-round

FLAVOR

Strong aromatic flavor with deep herbal, slightly bitter and warm notes

PROCESSING

Can be added to juices and smoothies, however most commonly used in wellness or flu shots due to its antifungal and antiviral qualities

CONTAINS

Not a significant source of vitamins or minerals

Papaya

SUB CATEGORY: **FRUIT**

HEALTH BENEFITS

Anti-inflammatory, antioxidant, helps with atherosclerosis, prevents some forms of cancer, improves cardiovascular health, lowers cholesterol, improves immune system, prevents diabetic heart disease, improves digestive system, helps with emphysema, improves heart health, prevents macular degeneration, helps prevent rheumatoid arthritis, promotes healthy skin, helps prevent stroke, prevents some forms of throat disease

FLAVOR PAIRING

Agave Nectar
Arugula
Avocado
Bell Pepper
Berries
Carrot
Cayenne
Chili Pepper
Cilantro
Cinnamon
Citrus
Coconut
Cucumber
Ginger
Grapefruit
Honey
Jicama
Kiwi
Lavender
Lettuce
Mango
Melon
Mint
Nutmeg
Nuts
Orange
Passion Fruit
Peach
Pineapple
Spinach
Vanilla
Yogurt

IDEAS

1. PAPAYA + LIME + MINT + YOGURT + HONEY
2. PAPAYA + ORANGE + BANANA + GUAVA + YOGURT
3. PAPAYA + LIME + MANGO + CAYENNE + AGAVE NECTAR + YOGURT

SEASON

Year-round, peaking summer through autumn

FLAVOR

Mildly sweet and slightly sour with musky notes of melon

PROCESSING

Due to its texture, papaya works best when either blended in a smoothie or blended with a liquid and then mixed into juice

CONTAINS

Vitamin C, Vitamin A, Vitamin B9-Folate, Vitamin E, Vitamin K

A B C D E F G H I J K L M N O P Q R S T U V W X Y Z

Parsley

SUB CATEGORY: **HERB**

— IN SEASON
— AVAILABLE
— LIMITED AVAILABILITY

HEALTH BENEFITS

Helps prevent diabetes, helps with rheumatoid arthritis, anti-inflammatory, strengthens the immune system, helps prevent some forms of cancer

FLAVOR PAIRING

Apple	Fennel	Sweet Potato
Avocado	Garlic	Tarragon
Basil	Ginger	Tomato
Beet	Greens	
Bell Pepper	Lemon	
Cabbage	Mint	
Carrot	Orange	
Chili Pepper	Pepper, Black	
Cilantro	Pine Nut	
Cucumber	Spinach	

IDEAS

1. PARSLEY + TOMATO + GARLIC + LIME + CELERY + SPINACH
2. PARSLEY + PINEAPPLE + JALAPEÑO + CILANTRO + JICAMA
3. PARSLEY + CUCUMBER + KALE + GINGER + LEMON + GREEN APPLE

SEASON

Year-round, especially in spring

FLAVOR

Earthy notes with hints of celery, lemon and pepper

PROCESSING

The stems contain a lot of flavor so be sure to add to juice

CONTAINS

Not a significant source of vitamins or minerals

Passion Fruit

SUB CATEGORY: **FRUIT**

IN SEASON
AVAILABLE
LIMITED AVAILABILITY

HEALTH BENEFITS

Prevents some forms of cancer, lowers blood pressure, improves eyesight, strengthens cardiovascular system, improves digestive system, improves mood, helps with asthma

FLAVOR PAIRING

Agave Nectar
Apple
Banana
Basil
Chili Pepper
Chocolate
Cinnamon
Citrus
Coconut
Ginger
Honey
Kiwi
Lime
Mango
Melon
Mint
Nuts
Papaya
Pineapple
Plum
Raspberry
Strawberry
Vanilla
Yogurt

IDEAS

1. PASSION FRUIT + COCONUT WATER
2. PASSION FRUIT + MANGO + LIME + YOGURT
3. PASSION FRUIT + ORANGE + PINEAPPLE + GINGER + MINT

SEASON

Winter through summer

FLAVOR

Sweet, sour and tart with hints of guava and honey

PROCESSING

Works best when passion fruit is cut in half, seeds scooped out and added to juice, also works great mixed with water, the crunchy seeds from the passion fruit will give the drink texture

CONTAINS

Vitamin A, Vitamin C

Pea, Snap

SUB CATEGORY: **VEGETABLE**

IN SEASON
AVAILABLE
LIMITED AVAILABILITY

HEALTH BENEFITS

Prevents Alzheimer's disease, prevents anemia, anti-inflammatory, antioxidant rich, prevents anxiety, prevents arthritis, lowers blood sugar, prevents some forms of cancer, strengthens cardiovascular system, prevents cataracts, lowers cholesterol, increases energy, improves eye health, strengthens heart health, improves immune system, prevents macular degeneration, improves memory, relieves stress, prevents strokes, prevents type 2 diabetes

FLAVOR PAIRING

Apple
Basil
Bell Pepper
Broccoli
Carrot
Chili Pepper
Cilantro
Fennel
Garlic
Ginger
Greens
Lettuce
Mint
Parsley
Pepper, Black
Tarragon
Yogurt

IDEAS

1. SNAP PEA + CARROT + FENNEL + LEMON
2. SNAP PEA + BROCCOLI + LIME+GINGER + CUCUMBER + PARSLEY
3. SNAP PEA + KALE + CUCUMBER + LEMON + GINGER + GREEN APPLE

SEASON

Year-round, peaking during the spring

FLAVOR

Sweet and fresh with slight grassy flavor

PROCESSING

Depending on the season, varieties of peas in the pod work best for juice such as sugar snap peas and snow peas. Add fresh crisp sweetness to juice.

CONTAINS

Vitamin K, Manganese, Vitamin C, Vitamin B1-thiamin, Vitamin A, Vitamin B9-Folate, Vitamin B6, Vitamin B3-Niacin, Magnesium, Vitamin B2-Riboflavin, Copper, Iron, Zinc, Choline

Peach

SUB CATEGORY: **FRUIT**

HEALTH BENEFITS

Antioxidant rich, prevents some forms of cancer, strengthens the heart, improves eye health

FLAVOR PAIRING

- Allspice
- Apple
- Apricot
- Arugula
- Basil
- Berries
- Cardamom
- Chili Pepper
- Chocolate
- Cilantro
- Cinnamon
- Cloves
- Coconut
- Fennel
- Ginger
- Grape
- Greens
- Hazelnut
- Honey
- Lavender
- Lemon
- Lemon Verbena
- Lime
- Lychee
- Mango
- Maple Syrup
- Mint
- Nutmeg
- Orange
- Pomegranate
- Stone Fruit
- Vanilla
- Watercress
- Yogurt
- Yuzu

IDEAS

1. PEACH + YUZU + PEAR + MINT + CUCUMBER
2. PEACH + RED APPLE + LEMON + GINGER + LAVENDER
3. PEACH + YOGURT + VANILLA + STRAWBERRY + HONEY

SEASON

Late spring through summer

FLAVOR

Sweet and slightly tart, with hints of honey

PROCESSING

Works great in smoothies for its texture, can also be blended in blender with a little liquid and mixed into juice, or can be juiced on its own - doesn't have a great yield due to its soft mushy texture but flavorful enough to infuse when mixed with other items

CONTAINS

Vitamin C, Vitamin A

Recipe

SWEET GREEN

INGREDIENTS

PINEAPPLE 54.1%
15 oz / 425 g

CUCUMBER 26.4%
7.3 oz / 207 g

GREEN APPLE 17.8%
5 oz / 142 g

MINT 1.8%
.49 oz / 14 g

BENEFITS

1. *Digestion booster*
2. *Immunity booster*

RECIPE YIELD

16 oz / 473 ml

FLAVOR PROFILE

SWEET — SAVORY

LIGHT — BOLD

FRUIT — VEGGIE

Pear

SUB CATEGORY: **FRUIT**

HEALTH BENEFITS

Anti-inflammatory, antioxidant rich, lowers blood pressure, prevents some forms of cancer, improves energy, strengthens immune system, improves lung health, prevents osteoporosis, helps with throat soreness, helps prevent some forms of diabetes

FLAVOR PAIRING

Agave Nectar	Cinnamon	Lemon	Persimmon
Allspice	Citrus	Lime	Pineapple
Apple	Cloves	Maple Syrup	Pomegranate
Arugula	Dates	Mint	Quince
Banana	Fennel	Nutmeg	Rhubarb
Blackberry	Figs	Nuts	Spinach
Cardamom	Ginger	Orange	Star Anise
Celery	Grapefruit	Parsley	Vanilla
Cherry	Greens	Passion Fruit	Watercress
Chocolate	Honey	Pepper, Black	

IDEAS

1. PEAR + BEET + LEMON + RED APPLE + GINGER
2. PEAR + GRAPEFRUIT + ORANGE + POMEGRANATE
3. PEAR + LIME + PINEAPPLE + JALAPEÑO + CILANTRO + JICAMA

SEASON

Year-round, especially autumn through winter

FLAVOR

Sweet with subtle notes of nuts and honey

PROCESSING

Adds subtle sweetness to juice blends without overpowering

CONTAINS

Vitamin C, Vitamin K

Pear, Asian

IN SEASON
AVAILABLE
LIMITED AVAILABILITY

SUB CATEGORY: FRUIT

HEALTH BENEFITS

Anti-inflammatory, antioxidant rich, lowers blood pressure, prevents some forms of cancer, improves energy, strengthens immune system, improves lung health, prevents osteoporosis, helps with throat soreness, helps prevent some forms of diabetes

FLAVOR PAIRING

Agave Nectar	Cinnamon	Lemon	Persimmon
Allspice	Citrus	Lime	Pineapple
Apple	Clove	Maple Syrup	Pomegranate
Arugula	Date	Mint	Quince
Banana	Fennel	Nutmeg	Rhubarb
Blackberry	Fig	Nuts	Spinach
Cardamom	Ginger	Orange	Star Anise
Celery	Grapefruit	Parsley	Vanilla
Cherry	Greens	Passion Fruit	Watercress
Chocolate	Honey	Pepper, Black	

IDEAS

1. ASIAN PEAR + LEMON + VANILLA
2. ASIAN PEAR + GINGER + LIME + GRAPEFRUIT
3. ASIAN PEAR + GREEN APPLE + PINEAPPLE + MINT

SEASON

Year-round

FLAVOR

Sweet, crisp taste with hints of honey and vanilla along with slight citrus notes

PROCESSING

Similar to other pear varieties, works well when being juiced, adds sweetness without overpowering other flavors

CONTAINS

Vitamin C, Vitamin K

Pecan

SUB CATEGORY: NUT

IN SEASON
AVAILABLE
LIMITED AVAILABILITY

HEALTH BENEFITS

Improves cardiovascular health, supports digestive system, promotes weight loss, lowers risk of breast cancer, improves bone strength, anti-inflammatory, lowers blood pressure, reduces risk for stroke, promotes healthy skin, prevents hair loss

FLAVOR PAIRING

Almond
Agave Nectar
Apple
Apricot
Banana
Berries
Carrot
Cherry
Chocolate
Cacao Nib
Cinnamon
Coconut
Coffee
Date
Fig
Ginger
Grape
Hazelnut
Honey
Lavender
Maple Syrup
Molasses
Peach
Pear
Pistachio
Raisin
Rose Water
Vanilla
Yogurt

IDEAS

1. PECAN + ALMOND MYLK + PUMPKIN
2. PECAN + ALMOND MYLK + MAPLE SYRUP + VANILLA
3. PECAN + ALMOND MYLK + PUMPKIN PUREE + CINNAMON + CLOVE + ALLSPICE

SEASON

Year-round, especially in autumn

FLAVOR

Slight sweet and bitter with light, buttery taste

PROCESSING

Works well in nut mylks, if toasted before being processed the pecans will add a deeper, slightly richer flavor to the mylk

CONTAINS

Thiamin, Iron, Vitamin B6, Manganese, Magnesium, Zinc, Copper

A B C D E F G H I J K L M N O **P** Q R S T U V W X Y Z

Persimmon

SUB CATEGORY: FRUIT

HEALTH BENEFITS

Lowers blood pressure, prevents constipation, improves immune system, strengthens eyesight, improves circulation, aids in digestion, anti-aging

FLAVOR PAIRING

Agave Nectar
Avocado
Banana
Cherry
Cinnamon
Clove
Fig
Ginger
Grapefruit
Grape
Honey
Kiwi
Lemon
Lime
Maple Syrup
Nutmeg
Nuts
Orange
Pear
Pineapple
Pomegranate
Sweet Potato
Vanilla
Yogurt
Yuzu

IDEAS

1. PERSIMMON + GRAPEFRUIT + GRAPE
2. PERSIMMON + GINGER + PEAR + LIME
3. PERSIMMON + YOGURT + HONEY + CINNAMON + FIG

SEASON

Autumn through winter

FLAVOR

Sweet with notes of cinnamon, honey and apricot

PROCESSING

Very soft in texture when ripe, best when peeled and blended with some liquid and mixed into juice or blended into a smoothie

CONTAINS

Vitamin C

Pine Nut

SUB CATEGORY: NUT

— IN SEASON
— AVAILABLE
— LIMITED AVAILABILITY

HEALTH BENEFITS

Supports heart health, improves immune system, increases energy, suppresses appetite, anti-aging, improves vision

FLAVOR PAIRING

Agave Nectar	Coconut	Molasses
Apple	Coffee	Peach
Apricot	Date	Pear
Banana	Fig	Pecan
Berries	Ginger	Pistachio
Carrot	Grape	Raisin
Cherry	Hazelnut	Rose Water
Chocolate	Honey	Vanilla
Cacao Nib	Lavender	Yogurt
Cinnamon	Maple Syrup	

IDEAS

1. PINE NUT + ALMOND MYLK + MAPLE SYRUP + VANILLA
2. PINE NUT + ALMOND MYLK + COFFEE + AGAVE NECTAR
3. PINE NUT + YOGURT + CACAO POWDER + HONEY + MINT

SEASON

Year-round

FLAVOR

Rich and buttery in flavor with slight sweetness

PROCESSING

Toasting before processing will intensify the flavor of the pine nut, can be added to nut mylk mixture or blended into smoothies

CONTAINS

Magnesium, Vitamin E, Vitamin K, Zinc, Copper, Iron

A B C D E F G H I J K L M N O P Q R S T U V W X Y Z

Pineapple

IN SEASON
AVAILABLE
LIMITED AVAILABILITY

SUB CATEGORY: **FRUIT**

HEALTH BENEFITS

Anti-inflammatory, antioxidant, prevents asthma, helps with atherosclerosis, prevents bronchitis, prevents some forms of cancer, prevents carpal tunnel syndrome, improves immune system, prevents diabetic heart disease, improves digestion, increases energy, prevents gout, prevents macular degeneration, prevents pneumonia, improves respiratory health, prevents rheumatoid arthritis

FLAVOR PAIRING

Avocado	Coconut	Lime	Star Anise
Banana	Cucumber	Mango	Sweet Potato
Basil	Ginger	Maple Syrup	Vanilla
Beet	Grapefruit	Melon	
Bell Pepper	Honey	Mint	
Berries	Jicama	Nutmeg	
Chili Pepper	Kiwi	Orange	
Chocolate	Kumquat	Papaya	
Cilantro	Lavender	Passion Fruit	
Cinnamon	Lemon	Rosemary	

IDEAS

1. **PINEAPPLE + PEAR + CILANTRO + JALAPEÑO**
2. **PINEAPPLE + GRAPEFRUIT + ORANGE + GINGER**
3. **PINEAPPLE + GREEN APPLE + MINT + CUCUMBER**

SEASON

Year-round, especially spring through summer

FLAVOR

Sweet and sour with acidic taste

PROCESSING

Very popular in juices and smoothies due to its balance of sweet and acidic flavors, does not juice well on centrifugal juicers due to being extremely fibrous

CONTAINS

Vitamin C, Manganese

Pistachio

SUB CATEGORY: NUT

IN SEASON
AVAILABLE
LIMITED AVAILABILITY

HEALTH BENEFITS

Improves heart health, improves immune system, helps with weight management, improves skin health, lowers cholesterol

FLAVOR PAIRING

Almond
Avocado
Cardamom
Cherry
Chocolate
Coconut
Cranberry
Date
Fig
Honey
Mango
Maple Syrup
Mint
Peach
Pineapple
Quince
Rose Water
Saffron
Vanilla

IDEAS

1. PISTACHIO + DATE + ALMOND MYLK + FIG
2. PISTACHIO + ALMOND MYLK + HONEY + ROSE WATER
3. PISTACHIO + CACAO POWDER + ALMOND MYLK + HONEY + MINT

SEASON

Year-round

FLAVOR

Rich in flavor with notes of butter

PROCESSING

Toasting right before processing helps bring out the flavor of the pistachio, works well being added to nut mylks and smoothies

CONTAINS

Fiber, Thiamin, Vitamin B6, Copper, Manganese

A B C D E F G H I J K L M N O P Q R S T U V W X Y Z

Plum

- IN SEASON
- AVAILABLE
- LIMITED AVAILABILITY

SUB CATEGORY: FRUIT

HEALTH BENEFITS

Anti-inflammatory, antioxidant, improves respiratory health, prevents atherosclerosis, prevents some forms of cancer, lowers cholesterol, improves heart health, prevents macular disease, improves immune system, helps with rheumatoid arthritis, helps prevent stroke, improves tissue health

FLAVOR PAIRING

Apple	Cinnamon	Nectarine
Apricot	Clove	Nuts
Arugula	Date	Orange
Banana	Ginger	Passion Fruit
Berries	Grapefruit	Peach
Cardamom	Honey	Pear
Cherry	Lemon	Rhubarb
Chili Pepper	Lime	Star Anise
Chocolate	Maple Syrup	Vanilla
Cilantro	Mint	Yogurt

IDEAS

1. PLUM + GRAPEFRUIT + MINT
2. PLUM + LIME + PEAR + GINGER
3. PLUM + BEET + ORANGE + CUCUMBER

SEASON

Summer through beginning of autumn

FLAVOR

Sweet and slightly sour with slight notes of cherries and citrus

PROCESSING

Needs to be deseeded before being processed, adds deep sweetness to smoothies and juices that pairs well with other stone fruits and berries

CONTAINS

Vitamin C

Pomegranate

SUB CATEGORY: **FRUIT**

HEALTH BENEFITS

Lowers blood pressure, prevents constipation, improves immune system, strengthens eyesight, improves circulation, aids in digestion, anti-aging

FLAVOR PAIRING

Agave Nectar
Allspice
Apple
Arugula
Avocado
Banana
Bell Pepper
Cardamom
Carrot
Cherry
Chili Pepper
Chocolate
Cinnamon
Clove
Coconut
Cranberry
Cucumber
Fig
Ginger
Grapefruit
Honey
Lemon
Lime
Maple Syrup
Melon
Mint
Orange
Pear
Quince
Spinach
Sweet Potato
Watermelon
Yogurt
Yuzu

IDEAS

1. POMEGRANATE + GINGER + LIME
2. POMEGRANATE + ORANGE + BEET
3. POMEGRANATE + WATERMELON + LIME

SEASON

Late autumn through winter

FLAVOR

Sour and sweet with notes of cranberries

PROCESSING

Arils can be added directly to juice for added texture, to juice you can either press with or without the skin on, if skin is processed too much when being juiced can give a slight off- taste

CONTAINS

Vitamin C

Pumpkin

SUB CATEGORY: **VEGETABLE**

— IN SEASON
— AVAILABLE
— LIMITED AVAILABILITY

HEALTH BENEFITS

Lowers blood pressure, sleep aid, supports heart health

FLAVOR PAIRING

Allspice
Apple
Basil
Cardamom
Carrot
Cashew
Cayenne
Chili Pepper
Chocolate
Cinnamon
Clove
Coconut
Cranberry
Fennel
Ginger
Hazelnut
Honey
Lemon
Lime
Maple Syrup
Mint
Molasses
Nutmeg
Nuts
Orange
Pear
Pecan
Pineapple
Vanilla
Walnut
Yogurt

IDEAS

1. PUMPKIN + GINGER + LEMON + PEAR + CAYENNE
2. PUMPKIN (PUREE) + ALMOND MYLK + MAPLE SYRUP + VANILLA
3. PUMPKIN + SWEET POTATO + RED APPLE + CINNAMON + NUTMEG + CLOVE + LEMON

SEASON

Autumn through mid-winter

FLAVOR

Sweet and earthy with notes of sweet potato

PROCESSING

A good process is actually using pumpkin puree and mixing into nut mylks or smoothies, use a high quality one, typically only contains roasted pumpkin puree and spices such as cinnamon, allspice and nutmeg, or juice fresh pumpkin, works best when peeled and de-seeded

CONTAINS

Vitamin A, Vitamin C

Recipe

HEAVY GREEN

INGREDIENTS

CUCUMBER 39.6%
10.8 oz / 306 g

SPINACH 19.8%
5.4 oz / 153 g

KALE 19.8%
5.4 oz / 153 g

CELERY 13.8%
3.8 oz / 107 g

LIME 6.9%
1.9 oz / 53 g

HIMALAYAN SALT 0.1%
.04 oz / 1 g

BENEFITS

1. *Antioxidant rich*
2. *Skin purifying*
3. *Reduces cholesterol*

RECIPE YIELD

16 oz / 473 ml

FLAVOR PROFILE

SWEET — SAVORY

LIGHT — BOLD

FRUIT — VEGGIE

Radish, Red

IN SEASON
AVAILABLE
LIMITED AVAILABILITY

SUB CATEGORY: **VEGETABLE, ROOT**

HEALTH BENEFITS

Clears sinuses, lowers blood pressure, relief from jaundice, assists with weight loss, aids in digestion

FLAVOR PAIRING

Agave Nectar
Apple
Bell Pepper
Bok Choy
Broccoli
Cabbage
Carrot
Cilantro
Cucumber
Daikon
Garlic
Ginger
Greens
Honey
Lemon
Lime
Pear
Scallion
Snow Pea
Wasabi

IDEAS

1. RADISH + TOMATO + GARLIC + CELERY + LIME + CARROT
2. RADISH + KALE + LEMON + GREEN APPLE + GINGER + CUCUMBER + CELERY
3. RADISH + ROMAINE + BOK CHOY + LIME + GINGER + BROCCOLI + GREEN APPLE

SEASON

Year-round especially spring through summer

FLAVOR

Fresh and crisp flavor with slight peppery heat

PROCESSING

Used mostly in juices for its health benefits, can add peppery notes when added to juice blends, pair different varieties of radish to adjust color of the juice being produced to achieve desired color

CONTAINS

Vitamin C

Raisin

SUB CATEGORY: **FRUIT, DRIED**

IN SEASON
AVAILABLE
LIMITED AVAILABILITY

HEALTH BENEFITS

Energy booster, aids in digestion, promotes heart and eye health, aids in healthy weight gain

SEASON

Year-round

FLAVOR PAIRING

Allspice
Almond
Apple
Apricot
Banana
Cardamom
Carrot
Cinnamon
Clove
Date
Ginger
Hazelnut
Honey
Lemon
Maple Syrup
Nutmeg
Nuts
Orange
Pear
Pecan
Pineapple
Pine Nut
Pistachio
Pumpkin
Sweet Potato
Vanilla
Walnut

FLAVOR

Sweet with deep notes of berries and honey

PROCESSING

Can be used as a sweet element in nut mylks and smoothies, best when soaked or re-hydrated before processing

CONTAINS

Vitamin B6, Iron

IDEAS

1. RAISIN + ALMOND MYLK + PUMPKIN
2. RAISIN + ALMOND MYLK + CACAO POWDER + HONEY
3. RAISIN + ALMOND MYLK + PUMPKIN PUREE + NUTMEG + CINNAMON + CLOVE + MAPLE SYRUP

Raspberry

SUB CATEGORY: FRUIT, BERRY

IN SEASON
AVAILABLE
LIMITED AVAILABILITY

HEALTH BENEFITS

Anti-inflammatory, antioxidant, helps prevent atherosclerosis, supports lowering blood sugar, helps prevent and slows cancer, assists weight loss, lowers risk of several chronic diseases including hypertension, Crohn's disease, type 2 diabetes, heart disease and Alzheimer's disease

FLAVOR PAIRING

Almond
Apple
Apricot
Banana
Berries
Chocolate
Cinnamon
Citrus
Clove
Fig
Ginger
Grapefruit
Grape
Hazelnut
Honey
Lemon
Lime
Mango
Maple Syrup
Melon
Mint
Nectarine
Nuts
Orange
Papaya
Peach
Pear
Pecan
Pineapple
Pistachio
Plum
Rhubarb
Star Anise
Vanilla
Watermelon
Yogurt

IDEAS

1. RASPBERRY + WATERMELON + ROSEMARY + LIME
2. RASPBERRY + ALMOND MYLK + CACAO POWDER + HONEY
3. RASPBERRY + ORANGES + GRAPEFRUIT + PINEAPPLE + MINT

SEASON

Year-round, especially summer

FLAVOR

Tart and sweet with delicate flavor

PROCESSING

Works well added to smoothies or blended into puree with liquid and mixed into juices, can also be used to alter the color and flavor of the juice, works well being added directly into finished juices to infuse flavor and texture

CONTAINS

Vitamin C, Manganese, Vitamin K

Rhubarb

SUB CATEGORY: VEGETABLE

- IN SEASON
- AVAILABLE
- LIMITED AVAILABILITY

HEALTH BENEFITS

Lowers blood pressure, prevents constipation, improves immune system, strengthens eyesight, improves circulation, aids in digestion, anti-aging

FLAVOR PAIRING

Almond	Coconut	Peach
Apple	Ginger	Pineapple
Apricot	Grapefruit	Plum
Banana	Honey	Pomegranate
Berries	Lemon	Raspberry
Cardamom	Lime	Rose Water
Celery	Mango	Star Anise
Cherry	Melon	Strawberry
Cinnamon	Mint	Vanilla
Citrus	Orange	Yogurt

IDEAS

1. RHUBARB + RED APPLE + ORANGE
2. RHUBARB + PINEAPPLE + LIME + GREEN APPLE + CUCUMBER
3. RHUBARB + STRAWBERRY + WATERMELON + ROSE WATER + MINT

SEASON

Spring and most of summer

FLAVOR

Tart and sour with notes of lemon

PROCESSING

Use only the stem when juicing, will add tartness and acidic taste to finished product

CONTAINS

Vitamin C

A B C D E F G H I J K L M N O P Q R S T U V W X Y Z

Rosemary

SUB CATEGORY: HERB

IN SEASON
AVAILABLE
LIMITED AVAILABILITY

HEALTH BENEFITS

Antibacterial, antiseptic properties, helps with memory, assists to combat cancer, prevents Alzheimer's, liver detoxifier and stress reliever

FLAVOR PAIRING

Apple
Apricot
Beet
Bell Pepper
Carrot
Celery
Citrus
Fennel
Garlic
Grapefruit
Grape
Honey
Lavender
Lemon
Lime
Mint
Orange
Parsley
Pear
Pepper Black
Pineapple
Spinach
Strawberry
Sweet Potato
Tomato

IDEAS

1. ROSEMARY + PEAR + LIME
2. ROSEMARY + WATERMELON
3. ROSEMARY + GRAPEFRUIT + ORANGE + PINEAPPLE

SEASON

Year-round

FLAVOR

Bitter and aromatic with hints of pine, pepper, sage and lemon

PROCESSING

Needles need to be removed from stem, the stem can become bitter if processed, typically rosemary is milder in the winter and stronger during the summer

CONTAINS

Vitamin C, Vitamin A

Spinach

SUB CATEGORY: **VEGETABLE, LETTUCE**

IN SEASON
AVAILABLE
LIMITED AVAILABILITY

HEALTH BENEFITS

Prevents anemia and acidosis, anti-inflammatory, antioxidant, helps prevent atherosclerosis and bleeding gums, promotes bone health, helps prevent cancer, promotes cardiovascular health, aids digestive health, improves eye health, blood pressure, increases mental awareness, helps prevent osteoporosis

FLAVOR PAIRING

Apple
Arugula
Avocado
Basil
Beet
Bell Pepper
Broccoli
Cayenne
Chili Pepper
Cilantro
Coconut
Clove
Cumin
Fig
Garlic
Ginger
Greens
Horseradish
Lemon
Lime
Mint
Nuts
Orange
Parsley
Pear
Pepper, Black
Pomegranate
Rosemary
Sweet Potato
Tangerine
Tarragon
Thyme
Tomato
Tomatillo
Yogurt
Yuzu

IDEAS

1. SPINACH + BEET + YUZU + GINGER
2. SPINACH + GRAPEFRUIT + ORANGES + MINT
3. SPINACH + TOMATO + GARLIC + LEMON + BELL PEPPER + CARROT + CELERY

SEASON

Year-round

FLAVOR

Lightly bitter and sweet with fresh grassy notes

PROCESSING

One of the mildest of the greens, packed with vitamins and nutrients and able to add a vibrant green color to most juices and smoothies

CONTAINS

Vitamin K, Vitamin A, Vitamin B9-Folate, Vitamin C, Manganese

A B C D E F G H I J K L M N O P Q R **S** T U V W X Y Z

Sprouts, Alfalfa

— IN SEASON
— AVAILABLE
— LIMITED AVAILABILITY

SUB CATEGORY: **VEGETABLE**

HEALTH BENEFITS

Reduces risk of breast cancer, minimizes menopause symptoms, lowers blood glucose levels and treats diabetes, antioxidant, anti-aging, combats cholesterol

FLAVOR PAIRING

Avocado
Bell Pepper
Cilantro
Ginger
Greens
Honey
Lemon
Lettuce
Lime
Mango
Orange
Sprouts
Sunflower Seed
Watercress

SEASON

Year-round

FLAVOR

Slightly sweet with nutty undertones

PROCESSING

Typically used for smoothies, can be added to juice blends to add distinct flavor

CONTAINS

Vitamin C, Vitamin K

IDEAS

1. ALFALFA SPROUTS + GINGER + LEMON + WHEATGRASS
2. ALFALFA SPROUTS + CARROT + GINGER + FENNEL + LEMON + RED APPLE
3. ALFALFA SPROUTS + GREEN APPLE + ROMAINE + LEMON + GINGER + CUCUMBER + CELERY

Squash, Butternut

SUB CATEGORY: **VEGETABLE**

HEALTH BENEFITS

Anti-inflammatory, antioxidant, lowers blood sugar, promotes cardiovascular health, helps prevent cancer, lowers cholesterol, promotes heart health, combats type 2 diabetes, wrinkle prevention

FLAVOR PAIRING

Allspice
Apple
Arugula
Basil
Berries
Cardamom
Carrot
Cayenne
Celery
Chili Pepper
Cilantro
Cinnamon
Clove
Coconut
Date
Fennel
Ginger
Greens
Honey
Kale
Lemon
Lime
Maple Syrup
Nutmeg
Nuts
Orange
Parsley
Pear
Pepper, Black
Pomegranate
Spinach
Star Anise
Thyme
Vanilla

IDEAS

1. BUTTERNUT SQUASH + RED APPLE + GINGER + LEMON
2. BUTTERNUT SQUASH + LEMON + SWEET POTATO + CAYENNE
3. BUTTERNUT SQUASH + PEAR + LIME + CILANTRO + JALAPEÑO

SEASON

Autumn through winter

FLAVOR

Sweet with hints of sweet potatoes and notes of butter

PROCESSING

Depending on the juicer, might need to be de-seeded and peeled before processing, when added to juice can add a deep sweetness to the blend

CONTAINS

Vitamin A, Vitamin C, Manganese, Vitamin B6, Potassium, Vitamin K, Vitamin B9-Folate

Star Anise

IN SEASON
AVAILABLE
LIMITED AVAILABILITY

SUB CATEGORY: **SPICE, SEED**

HEALTH BENEFITS

Helps with asthma, aids digestion, improves bad breath, supports immune system, antioxidant

FLAVOR PAIRING

Apple
Berries
Chocolate
Cacao Nib
Cinnamon
Citrus
Ginger
Mint
Pear
Plum
Rose Water
Molasses

IDEAS

1. STAR ANISE + RED APPLE + CINNAMON
2. STAR ANISE + BERRIES + HONEY + YOGURT
3. STAR ANISE + ALMOND MYLK + CHOCOLATE

SEASON

Year-round

FLAVOR

Aromatic spice with pungent notes of sweet licorice, slightly bitter and sweet

PROCESSING

Lightly toast to bring out flavor, can be steeped in liquid to extract flavor

CONTAINS

Not a significant source of vitamins or minerals

Strawberry

SUB CATEGORY: **FRUIT, BERRY**

HEALTH BENEFITS

Helps prevent Alzheimer's disease, anti-anemic, anti-inflammatory, antioxidant, lowers blood sugar, promotes brain health, prevents and combats cancer, lowers cholesterol, coagulant, promotes digestive health, diuretic, promotes heart health, strengthens immune system, improves mental health

FLAVOR PAIRING

Agave Nectar
Almond
Apple
Arugula
Banana
Basil
Bell Pepper
Berries
Chocolate
Cinnamon
Coconut
Cucumber
Fennel
Fig
Ginger
Grapefruit
Guava
Hazelnut
Honey
Kiwi
Lemon
Lime
Lychee
Mango
Maple Syrup
Melon
Mint
Nuts
Orange
Passion Fruit
Peach
Pineapple
Rhubarb
Spinach
Vanilla
Watermelon

IDEAS

1. STRAWBERRY + WATERMELON + BASIL + CUCUMBER
2. STRAWBERRY + BANANA + YOGURT + HONEY + VANILLA
3. STRAWBERRY + KIWI + LIME + CUCUMBER + MINT + ORANGE

SEASON

Year-round, peaking spring through summer

FLAVOR

Sweet and sour berry flavor

PROCESSING

Does not yield too much juice due to its soft flesh, works best when pureed with a little liquid and mixed into juice, the green tops can be used as long as washed thoroughly, it is a good way to add some nutrients and vitamins to the end product

CONTAINS

Vitamin C, Manganese

Recipe

SWEET POTATO SPICE

INGREDIENTS

SWEET POTATO 41.5%
14.4 oz / 408 g

PINEAPPLE 41.5%
14.4 oz / 408 g

ORANGE 15.2%
5.3 oz / 150 g

GINGER 1.5%
.53 oz / 15 g

CINNAMON 0.1%
.05 oz / 1 g

NUTMEG 0.1%
.05 oz / 1 g

CLOVE 0.1%
.05 oz / 1 g

BENEFITS

1. *Promotes healthy heart*
2. *Antioxidant rich*
3. *Digestion booster*

RECIPE YIELD

16 oz / 473 ml

FLAVOR PROFILE

SWEET — SAVORY

LIGHT — BOLD

FRUIT — VEGGIE

Sweet Potato

SUB CATEGORY: **VEGETABLE, ROOT**

HEALTH BENEFITS

Anti-inflammatory, antioxidant, stabilizes blood sugar levels, helps prevent cancer, improves digestion, fights lung cancer and emphysema, promotes heart health, boosts immune system, prevents muscle cramps, reduces stress, superfood for those with ulcerative colitis

FLAVOR PAIRING

Agave Nectar	Celery	Kale	Rosemary
Allspice	Chili Pepper	Lemon	Turmeric
Apple	Cilantro	Lime	Vanilla
Apricot	Cinnamon	Nutmeg	Watercress
Arugula	Cacao Powder	Nuts	
Basil	Coconut	Orange	
Bell Pepper	Fennel	Parsley	
Cardamom	Fig	Pear	
Carrot	Ginger	Pepper, Black	
Cayenne	Greens	Pineapple	

IDEAS

1. SWEET POTATO + PINEAPPLE + LIME + GINGER
2. SWEET POTATO + RED APPLE + LEMON + CINNAMON
3. SWEET POTATO + PEAR + ORANGE + PEPPER, BLACK + TURMERIC

SEASON

Year-round, especially autumn through winter

FLAVOR

Deep earthy sweetness with hints of pumpkin with a slight nutty flavor

PROCESSING

When juiced, gives a deep sweet flavor to the blend, keep the peel on when processing for its nutrients

CONTAINS

Vitamin A, Manganese, Vitamin B6, Potassium, Vitamin B5, Pantothenic Acid

Tarragon

IN SEASON
AVAILABLE
LIMITED AVAILABILITY

SUB CATEGORY: **HERB**

HEALTH BENEFITS

Antioxidant, supports cardiovascular health, prevents growth of cancer cells, maintains blood sugar levels, promotes digestive health, sleep aid, toothache remedy

FLAVOR PAIRING

Apple
Beet
Broccoli
Carrot
Citrus
Cucumber
Fennel
Grapefruit
Lemon
Lime
Melon
Mint
Orange
Parsley
Peach
Spinach
Snap Pea
Tomato

IDEAS

1. TARRAGON + ORANGE + BEETS + CUCUMBER
2. TARRAGON + GREEN APPLE + WATERMELON + LIME
3. TARRAGON + SPINACH + LEMON + CUCUMBER + FENNEL + GINGER

SEASON

Year-round

FLAVOR

Strong herbal notes of basil, anise, licorice and lemon

PROCESSING

Used sparingly in juice, it can add another layer of flavor to the blend, typically works with medium green juice blends through semi-sweet fruit based flavors, when processing be sure to use stems along with the leaves

CONTAINS

Magnesium, Iron, Zinc, Calcium, Vitamin A, Vitamin C

Thyme

SUB CATEGORY: **HERB**

— IN SEASON
— AVAILABLE
— LIMITED AVAILABILITY

HEALTH BENEFITS

Natural diuretic, appetite stimulant, antioxidant, prevents fungal and viral infections, improves circulation, protects heart, boosts immunity, reduces stress, treats respiratory issues

FLAVOR PAIRING

Apple
Basil
Beet
Bell Pepper
Carrot
Citrus
Fennel
Garlic
Lemon
Lettuce
Lime
Melon
Orange
Pear
Pepper, Black
Snap Pea
Spinach
Tomato
Watermelon

IDEAS

1. THYME + PEAR + ORANGE + FENNEL
2. THYME + WATERMELON + GREEN APPLE
3. THYME + SPINACH + CUCUMBER + LEMON + GINGER + CELERY + GREEN APPLE

SEASON

Year-round

FLAVOR

Bitter, sweet and earthy notes with slight hints of pine, citrus and caraway

PROCESSING

If the thyme is young the stem will be soft and be able to be processed, if it matures the stem will become woody and give a bitter taste when processed, works well when tiny leaves are picked and added directly to juice once processed

CONTAINS

Vitamin C, Vitamin A, Iron, Copper, Manganese

A B C D E F G H I J K L M N O P Q R S T U V W X Y Z

Tomato

IN SEASON
AVAILABLE
LIMITED AVAILABILITY

SUB CATEGORY: FRUIT

HEALTH BENEFITS

Fights anemia, anti-inflammatory, antioxidant, helps prevent atherosclerosis, promotes bone health, cancer fighting, promotes cardiovascular health, lowers cholesterol, promotes healthy digestion, fights fatigue, promotes heart health, strengthens immune system, supports kidneys and liver, reduces risk of neurological disease, promotes weight loss, improves skin

FLAVOR PAIRING

Arugula	Cucumber	Parsley
Avocado	Cumin	Pepper, Black
Beet	Fennel	Pumpkin
Bell Pepper	Garlic	Rosemary
Cayenne	Ginger	Snap Pea
Celery	Greens	Spinach
Chili Pepper	Lemon	Tarragon
Cilantro	Lime	Thyme
Cinnamon	Mint	Turmeric
Coriander	Oregano	Watermelon

IDEAS

1. TOMATO + ARUGULA + THYME + WATERMELON
2. TOMATO + SPINACH + LIME + FENNEL + CUCUMBER
3. TOMATO + GARLIC + BELL PEPPER + CELERY + KALE + CARROT + LEMON

SEASON

Year-round, peaking through summer

FLAVOR

Sweet and slightly acidic with deep earthy notes

PROCESSING

Works well in blends giving a deep, earthy, well balanced, sweet and acidic flavor, use salt to bring out full flavor of the tomato in juices, technically a fruit, most classify the tomato into the vegetable category due to its nutritional content and flavor

CONTAINS

Vitamin C, Vitamin A, Vitamin K, Potassium, Molybdenum, Manganese

Turmeric

- IN SEASON
- AVAILABLE
- LIMITED AVAILABILITY

SUB CATEGORY: **VEGETABLE, ROOT**

HEALTH BENEFITS

Natural diuretic, appetite stimulant, antioxidant, prevents fungal and viral infections, improves circulation, protects heart, boosts immunity, reduces stress, treats respiratory issues

FLAVOR PAIRING

Carrot
Chili Pepper
Cilantro
Cinnamon
Clove
Coconut
Cumin
Ginger
Greens
Lemon
Lime
Pepper, Black
Spinach
Sweet Potato

IDEAS

1. TURMERIC + LEMON + GINGER
2. TURMERIC + RED APPLE + GINGER + LIME + CAYENNE
3. TURMERIC + COCONUT WATER + LIME + GINGER + PEAR

SEASON

Year-round

FLAVOR

Earthy flavor slightly sweet with notes of ginger and orange

PROCESSING

Fresh turmeric should be processed very similar to ginger, if fresh is not available turmeric powder is a good substitute, turmeric is very popular in juicing due to its many health benefits, nutrients and vitamins

CONTAINS

Manganese, Iron, Vitamin B6, Potassium, Vitamin C, Magnesium

A B C D E F G H I J K L M N O P Q R S T U V W X Y Z

Turnip

SUB CATEGORY: VEGETABLE, ROOT

IN SEASON
AVAILABLE
LIMITED AVAILABILITY

HEALTH BENEFITS

Can help reduce intestinal issues, reduces inflammation, lowers blood pressure, can lower the risk of cancer, promotes a healthy digestive tract, regulates blood sugar levels

FLAVOR PAIRING

Allspice
Anise
Apple
Basil
Broccoli
Cabbage
Carrot
Celery
Chili Pepper
Cilantro
Cinnamon
Citrus
Ginger
Greens
Kale
Parsley
Pear
Pea
Radish
Root Vegetables
Sweet Potato
Tarragon
Tomato
Watercress

IDEAS

1. TURNIP + CARROT + RED APPLE + FENNEL + ORANGE
2. TURNIP + KALE + CELERY + GINGER + LEMON + CUCUMBER
3. TURNIP + TOMATO + LIME + GARLIC + CELERY + SALT + PEPPER + CUCUMBER

SEASON

Year-round especially autumn through winter

FLAVOR

Slightly sweet with pungent notes of mustard and pepper

PROCESSING

Turnips are packed with nutrients and vitamins, can use the bulb as well as the turnip greens for juicing, adds distinctive spice when incorporated with juices, can be used mostly for savory juices as well as some sweeter varietes with root vegetable baes such as carrots and beets

CONTAINS

Vitamin C

Vanilla

SUB CATEGORY: **VEGETABLE, ROOT**

— IN SEASON
— AVAILABLE
— LIMITED AVAILABILITY

HEALTH BENEFITS

Antioxidant, anti-inflammatory, mental health booster, may reduce fever, exhibits antibacterial properties

FLAVOR PAIRING

Apple	Clove	Pepper, Black
Apricot	Coffee	Pumpkin
Banana	Ginger	Raspberry
Beet	Honey	Strawberry
Berries	Lemon	Yogurt
Cardamom	Maple Syrup	
Cherry	Nutmeg	
Chili Pepper	Nuts	
Cacao Powder	Peach	
Cinnamon	Pear	

IDEAS

1. VANILLA + PEAR + LEMON
2. VANILLA + ALMOND MYLK + COFFEE + HONEY
3. VANILLA + DATE + ALMOND + MAPLE SYRUP + PUMPKIN PUREE

SEASON

Year-round

FLAVOR

Aromatic with rich notes of cream and light smoke

PROCESSING

Typically paired with nut mylks but also can add dimension to smoothies and juices, fresh from the pod is always recommended over an extract, to extract seed easily from the pod, microwave for 2 seconds on high or slightly warm, this will soften the pod making it easier to scrape out

CONTAINS

Not a significant source of vitamins or minerals

Walnut

SUB CATEGORY: NUT

IN SEASON
AVAILABLE
LIMITED AVAILABILITY

HEALTH BENEFITS

Helps to prevent heart disease, antioxidant, supports brain health, supports a healthy colon, aids in depression, fights inflammation

FLAVOR PAIRING

Agave Nectar	Cinnamon	Maple Syrup
Almond	Coconut	Molasses
Apple	Coffee	Peach
Apricot	Date	Pear
Banana	Fig	Pecan
Berries	Ginger	Pistachio
Carrot	Grape	Raisin
Cherry	Hazelnut	Rose Water
Chocolate	Honey	Vanilla
Cacao Nib	Lavender	Yogurt

IDEAS

1. WALNUT + DATE + COFFEE + AGAVE NECTAR + VANILLA
2. WALNUT + ALMOND + PUMPKIN PUREE + MAPLE SYRUP
3. WALNUT + ALMOND + RASPBERRY + CACAO POWDER + HONEY

SEASON

Year-round especially in autumn

FLAVOR

Slightly sweet and bitter with rich and astringent notes

PROCESSING

Works well for adding flavor to nut mylks, when processing try to avoid the skin, most of the astringent flavor from the walnut is in its skin

CONTAINS

Protein, Vitamin B6, Vitamin C, Magnesium, Phosphorous, Copper, Manganese, Omega-3

Watercress

IN SEASON
AVAILABLE
LIMITED AVAILABILITY

SUB CATEGORY: **VEGETABLE, LETTUCE**

HEALTH BENEFITS

Boosts immunity, cancer preventive for lung, breast and stomach cancer, lowers blood pressure, improves thyroid gland function, promotes weight loss, maintains healthy bones, improves vision, strengthens teeth, promotes brain health, prevents colds

FLAVOR PAIRING

Apple
Avocado
Beet
Bell Pepper
Carrot
Chili Pepper
Cilantro
Citrus
Cucumber
Fennel
Garlic
Ginger
Grapefruit
Greens
Horseradish
Jicama
Lemon
Lime
Mint
Orange
Parsley
Peach
Pear
Pineapple
Pomegranate
Raspberry
Snap Pea
Strawberry
Tangerine
Tomato

IDEAS

1. WATERCRESS + WATERMELON + STRAWBERRY + LIME
2. WATERCRESS + PINEAPPLE + JICAMA + MINT + ORANGE
3. WATERCRESS + KALE + GINGER + LEMON + CELERY + CUCUMBER

SEASON

Year-round especially late spring through summer

FLAVOR

Bitter and grassy with notes of pepper and mustard

PROCESSING

Can be used in both smoothies and juices, adds peppery notes to finished product

CONTAINS

Vitamin A, Vitamin C, Vitamin K

A B C D E F G H I J K L M N O P Q R S T U V W X Y Z

Watermelon

- IN SEASON
- AVAILABLE
- LIMITED AVAILABILITY

SUB CATEGORY: **FRUIT, MELON**

HEALTH BENEFITS

Anti-inflammatory, antioxidant, cardiovascular health, arthritis, bladder health, reduces blood pressure, cancer fighting, reduces cholesterol levels, hydrating, promotes heart health and skin health

FLAVOR PAIRING

Agave Nectar
Arugula
Basil
Berries
Chili Pepper
Chili Powder
Cilantro
Cucumber
Fennel
Ginger
Honey
Jicama
Lemon
Lime
Maple Syrup
Melon
Mint
Orange
Parsley
Pepper, Black
Rosemary
Tomato
Vanilla

IDEAS

1. WATERMELON + RASPBERRY + ROSEMARY
2. WATERMELON + GREEN APPLE + MINT + JALAPEÑO
3. WATERMELON + BASIL + FENNEL + LEMON + BLACK PEPPER

SEASON

Year-round, peaking through summer

FLAVOR

Very sweet and refreshing flavor with light floral notes

PROCESSING

Flavor pairing both juices and smoothies, the rind is packed with nutrients, can be juiced with the flesh, however this will change the color and mellow out the sweetness of the melon, if watermelon flesh is light in color, you can process a small piece of red beet with the watermelon to bring out a more vibrant color

CONTAINS

Vitamin C, Vitamin K

Recipe

SPICY WATERMELON

INGREDIENTS

WATERMELON 88%
19.2 oz / 544 g

GREEN APPLE 7.1%
1.6 oz / 44 g

RED BEET 2.2%
.48 oz / 14 g

LIME 1.4%
.31 oz / 9 g

MINT 0.7%
.14 oz / 4 g

JALAPEÑO 0.6%
.12 oz / 3 g

BENEFITS

1. *Hydrating*
2. *Metabolism booster*
3. *Cardiovascular support*

RECIPE YIELD

16 oz / 473 ml

FLAVOR PROFILE

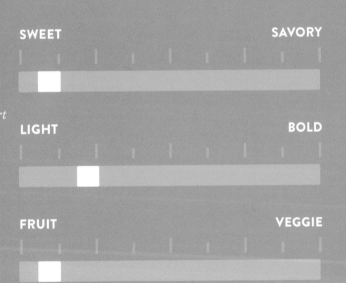

SWEET — SAVORY

LIGHT — BOLD

FRUIT — VEGGIE

Wheatgrass

SUB CATEGORY: **VEGETABLE**

IN SEASON
AVAILABLE
LIMITED AVAILABILITY

HEALTH BENEFITS

Antioxidant, improves cholesterol levels, reduces oxidative damage to cells, may help kill cancer cells, blood sugar regulation, alleviates inflammation, promotes weight loss

FLAVOR PAIRING

Apple
Arugula
Avocado
Basil
Beet
Bell Pepper
Bok Choy
Cabbage
Carrot
Celery
Chard
Chili Pepper
Cilantro
Garlic
Grapefruit
Greens
Kale
Lemon
Mint
Nuts
Orange
Oregano
Parsley
Snow Pea
Spinach
Sweet Potato
Tomato
Walnut

IDEAS

1. WHEATGRASS + LEMON
2. WHEATGRASS + ORANGE
3. WHEATGRASS + GINGER + CAYENNE + LIME

SEASON

Year-round

FLAVOR

Bright and pungent grassy flavor

PROCESSING

Typically served as a shot due to strong taste, wheatgrass is loaded with vitamins and nutrients

CONTAINS

Vitamin E, Vitamin B-5

Yuzu

SUB CATEGORY: **CITRUS**

— IN SEASON
— AVAILABLE
— LIMITED AVAILABILITY

HEALTH BENEFITS

Natural antibiotic, anti-inflammatory, antioxidant, prevents asthma, prevents atherosclerosis, prevents some forms of cancer, strengthens immune system, improves digestion, prevents heartburn, strengthens heart health, prevents rheumatoid arthritis, promotes healthy skin, prevents stroke

FLAVOR PAIRING

Arugula
Avocado
Basil
Beet
Bell Pepper
Berries
Broccoli
Cardamom
Carrot
Chocolate
Coconut
Cucumber
Fennel
Garlic
Greens
Ginger
Guava
Honey
Kale
Lavender
Lime
Mango
Maple Syrup
Mint
Nuts
Orange
Papaya
Parsley
Peach
Pear
Snap Pea
Tomato
Vanilla

IDEAS

1. YUZU + BEETS + GINGER + PEAR
2. YUZU + CARROT + APPLE + GINGER
3. YUZU + WATER + PEAR + ROSEMARY

SEASON

Peak autumn through winter

FLAVOR

Strong lemon flavor with herbal notes

PROCESSING

If fresh is not available, typically can be found pre-juiced in bottles, typically works better as substitute for citrus elements in juices and smoothies

CONTAINS

Vitamin C

BOOSTERS + ADDITIVES

ACAI POWDER

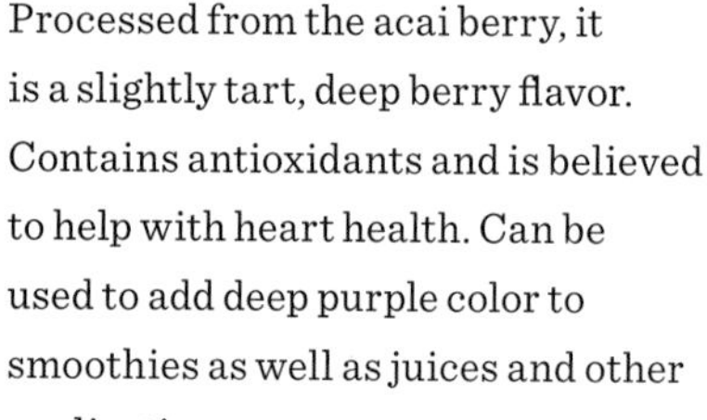

Processed from the acai berry, it is a slightly tart, deep berry flavor. Contains antioxidants and is believed to help with heart health. Can be used to add deep purple color to smoothies as well as juices and other applications.

AGAVE NECTAR

Sweetener made from the agave plant, sold typically as dark or light ambers as well as raw varieties, slightly sweeter than white granulated sugar with hints of caramel.

ALOE VERA

Gel is extracted from the aloe plant, can be used sparingly in juices, very mild in flavor and believed to have hydration benefits as well as being high in alkalinity to balance your body's pH.

ASHWAGANDHA ROOT

This root is often available in powder form and is believed to relieve stress and boost brain activity, works well when added to nut mylks and smoothies.

BEE POLLEN

This form of pollen is mild and lightly floral, can be added to juices, mylks and smoothies. Contains vitamins, amino acids and protein - also believed to help with allergies.

CACAO

Extracted from the cacao bean, loaded with antioxidants and fiber, typically used in smoothies to give a chocolate flavor without the sweetness of processed chocolate. Typically, the powder is used for nut mylks and smoothies. The nibs can be used for smoothies as well as other applications.

CAMU CAMU

This fruit can be found typically in powder form, contains large amounts of vitamin C and can be added to give juice and smoothies a citrus element.

CAYENNE

Powder made from the cayenne chili jump starts metabolism as well as adds heat when added to juices and smoothies. Cayenne does not dissolve completely, so it is best to either add small amounts to individual portions or use the liquid variety.

CHAGA MUSHROOM POWDER

A fungus known as the "king of medicinal mushrooms," it has an earthy flavor with slight bitter notes. High in ORAC value (oxygen radical absorbent capacity) and ability to fight free radicals. This powder can be added to smoothies and can work in some nut mylks as well.

CHARCOAL, ACTIVATED

Typically made from coconut. Used as a detox to remove toxins from the system due to the porous texture of charcoal. Gives juices and smoothies a deep black color. It is recommended to use a plastic or wooden spoon when handling, due to the possibility of removing toxins from metal spoons.

CHIA SEED

Hydrophilic seed that can absorb up to 12 times its weight in liquid, rich in omega-3 fatty acids and fiber, when added to juices can be used to add texture as well as nutritional benefits, can also be used as a natural vegan thickener and binder for applications such as puddings and granola.

CHLORELLA

Type of algae, packed with protein, dietary fiber and other nutrients, typically added to green juices in either powder or liquid form.

CHLOROPHYLL

Used in juices, most commonly the green variety for hydration benefits. Earthy and grassy in flavor.

CINNAMON

Cinnamon is produced from the bark of certain trees. Typically used in juices and smoothies on the sweeter side to add depth and light spice. Most common variety is cassia however the more rare Ceylon variety is believed to be more nutrient dense.

COCONUT PALM SUGAR

Natural sweetener made from the sap of a coconut palm, with hints of coconut flavor and slight notes of caramel.

COLLAGEN

Made from animal byproducts, collagen is believed to have hydration benefits as well as promote skin and bone health. The flavor is typically neutral.

DANDELION ROOT POWDER

Made from the dandelion root, this powder is known to remove toxins and believed to be a blood purifier.

E3 LIVE

Also known as blue-green algae, highly concentrated with vitamins, minerals, amino and fatty acids, has a slight deep grassy taste. Should be lightly used and mixed with other strong flavors, typically green in variety.

ECHINACEA EXTRACT

Extract made from the herb, is believed to strengthen the immune system.

FENUGREEK

Herb with slight nutty taste with hints of maple and celery. Typically found in seed and powder form. Contains iron as well as promotes healthy skin and hair.

FLAXSEED

Seed from the flax plant sometimes referred to as linseed, contains high amounts of omega-3 fatty acids, which can lead to cardiovascular health and help with blood pressure.

GINSENG

Extract made from the ginseng root, most commonly in either dried powder or liquid extract forms. Believed to boost energy, lower blood sugar levels and relieve stress.

GOJI BERRY

Sometimes referred to as a wolfberry, goji is a fruit from the nightshade family typically found in a dried form. Relatively high in vitamin A, vitamin C, and iron. They can be added directly to juice or smoothies to infuse flavor and/or add texture.

GUARANA POWDER

From the Guarana shrub, this powder is popular in Brazil and is used to reduce fatigue.

HEMP SEED

Seeds from the hemp plant, they can be soaked and used to make hemp mylk or added as is to juices or smoothies. They have a slight nutty flavor and are a great source for protein, vitamin E and many other minerals

HONEY

Natural sweetener produced by bees, can be added to most juices, smoothies or any other application for deep sweet flavor with floral notes that vary in taste. When using honey, it is best to use local due to its ability to assist with allergies for the area.

HONEY, MANUKA

Manuka honey is harvested in New Zealand from bees pollinating the manuka bush. Considered to have a much higher level of enzymes than regular honey, and has different health benefits than regular honey - such as promoting healthy skin and internal health. A "Unique Manuka Factor" (UMF), is used to show the concentration level of antibacterial strength in manuka honey.

KELP, POWDER

Produced from underwater kelp plants, with a slightly salty and umami taste, powdered kelp typically works best with other green juices and smoothies. Contains a large amount of iodine.

MACA, POWDER

Produced from a root and then dried into powder form, maca powder has a mild taste with slight hints of butterscotch, can be used in almost all smoothies for its neutral taste as well as some mylks and juices. Believed to boost energy and be a mood enhancer.

MAJIK (BLUE SPIRULINA)

Produced from spirulina, this powder has all the benefits of spirulina but with an extremely vibrant blue color, some might have a slight fishy smell, however only a little is needed per serving. Works well with light colored smoothies and juices as well as most nut mylks.

MAPLE SYRUP

Produced by reducing the sap from maple trees, works well in smoothies, juices and lemonades for an added sweetness. The darker the shade of amber, the deeper the flavor.

MATCHA, POWDER

Produced from green tea leaves, matcha has a slight earthy and grassy flavor. Loaded with antioxidants as well as a rich source of chlorophyll.

MAQUI, POWDER

Produced from the maqui berry popular in Chile, is considered an antioxidant rich superfood, contains high levels of potassium, iron and fiber. With deep berry flavor, it works well in smoothies and lighter to sweeter juice blends.

MORINGA

Produced from the moringa tree leaves, the flavor is slight grassy and nutty. Can be added to most smoothies and juices, it is considered a nutrient powerhouse as well as contains fiber and protein.

OIL, BLACK CUMIN SEED

Oil made from the black cumin seed, this oil is very strong in flavor and should be used sparingly. With vitamins A, B and C it is believed to have many benefits including boosting your immune system, as well as promoting healthy hair. Works well when used in savory juices and shots.

OIL, CBD

Cannabidiol oil or CBD oil for short is derived from the cannabis plant. Believed to help reduce pain, relieve stress and reduce inflammation.

OIL, COCONUT

Produced from the meat of the coconut. Has a coconut taste and rich with nutrients. Believed to promote healthy skin and hair. Best when used in smoothies, can be used in mylks, however will solidify if left at cooler temperatures.

OIL, EVENING PRIMROSE

Oil produced from the primrose flower seeds, evening primrose oil is a good source of essential fatty acids and it is believed to decrease inflammation and assist with arthritis.

OIL, FLAXSEED

See Flaxseed

OIL, HEMP

See Hemp Seeds

OIL, OREGANO

Oil produced from the oregano herb, the oil carries a strong flavor of oregano. Most commonly used to strengthen the immune system, works well in shots and sparingly in savory smoothies and juices.

OIL, PEPPERMINT

Produced from the peppermint herb, a cross between mint and spearmint, the oil has similar strong flavors of both. Believed to help mostly with upset stomachs, some take this to assist with headache relief, common cold and nausea.

PROBIOTICS

Microorganisms sometimes referred to as bacteria, probiotics are most known for promoting gut health as well as helping the body function properly.

PROTEIN POWDER

Most commonly made from either whey, soy or pea protein. Works best with smoothies and nut mylks. Can be used to add a boost of protein.

REISHI MUSHROOM POWDER

Made from the Reishi mushroom, this powder is believed to reduce anxiety as well as boost the immune system. Works well in nut mylks and smoothies for its mild, slightly sweet flavor - especially works well with cacao.

SALT, PINK HIMALAYAN

A variation of salt produced from a region of Pakistan, pink Himalayan salt is believed to have slightly higher mineral content compared to traditional sea salt. Works well in juices, smoothies and mylks especially to help balance out sweetness or to bring out flavors.

Some of these products or claims have not been scientifically proven to treat, cure, or prevent any disease. Always make sure when selecting supplements that they are approved for food use by the FDA and/or local health department.

SEA BUCKTHORN

From the sea buckthorn berry, found in all forms - fresh, extract and powder. Has a tangy citrus flavor, the sea buckthorn contains large amounts of vitamin C as well as high levels of vitamin E and antioxidants. Works well with other citruses in most applications.

SORGHUM

Sweetener produced from sorghum grass, has a similar taste to molasses and is often called sorghum molasses. Contains iron, calcium and potassium. Works well as a sweetening agent for mylks, lemonades and smoothies.

SPIRULINA

Also known as blue-green algae, highly concentrated with vitamins, minerals, amino and fatty acids, has a slight deep grassy taste, should be lightly used and mixed with other strong flavors, typically green in variety.

TRIPHALA POWDER

Triphala is an ancient ayurvedic herb and staple, it is very bitter and astringent, it combines three fruits: alma berry, haritaki, and bibhitaki. It's most commonly known for its cancer fighting ability. Works great for bowels and/or to strengthen intestinal muscles as well as a colon cleanser. Can be incorporated into smoothies, mylks and juices.

TURMERIC POWDER

Produced from the turmeric root, this powder, produces a vibrant yellow color when added to any item Turmeric powder is fragrant and has slight hints of spicy mustard and ginger. Most commonly used for its anti-inflammatory qualities, it can be added to smoothies, juices and much more.

VANILLA

Pods produced from the vanilla flower, can be found in either fresh, powder or extract form. Vanilla has a very sweet and floral aroma. Works best with smoothies, mylks as well as some sweeter varieties of juices.

VINEGAR, APPLE CIDER

Produced from apples, this vinegar has many benefits including antibacterial, anti-inflammatory and even can relieve a sore throat and prevent bad breath. Best to use raw and unfiltered when available, typically added to juices or shots.

WHEATGRASS POWDER

Produced from wheatgrass, this product will have all the benefits of wheatgrass. It can be added to most smoothies and juices however pairs best with the green varieties.

ZEOLITE

Is a mineral found in powder form. Used to remove toxins from the body. Works best when used in liquids such as juices, lemonades and mylks where it is left to hydrate for 8 hours before consuming.

IT'S NOT JUST A RECIPE BOOK • IT'S AN IDEA BOOK •